"Alicia Cola:, a twelve-year-old girl, was
making her bed before going to school one
morning. As she shook out the sheets,
a rat fell from her bed. She was frightened
and ran from the room screaming. Her
father simply brought plaster and covered
a crack in the wall through which the
animal had come into the apartment."

—from *Up from Puerto Rico*
by Elena Padilla

What happens to the people who must live in a slum?
How can we relieve their misery and rebuild our cities? Fifteen writers, sociologists, and residents of the
inner city attack the problem of slum housing.

Included are selections by Jacob K. Javits, James
Baldwin, Daniel Patrick Moynihan, and Whitney M.
Young, Jr.

PROBLEMS OF AMERICAN SOCIETY

Focusing on the urban scene, youth, the individual and his search for a better life, the books in this series probe the most crucial dilemmas of our time.

The Negro in the City
Civil Rights and Civil Liberties
Crime and Juvenile Delinquency
Poverty and the Poor
Air and Water Pollution
The Traffic Jam
The Slums
*The City as a Community
*City Government
*The Draft
*The People of the City
*The Consumer
*Drugs
*Riots

*Forthcoming

GERALD LEINWAND

assisted by
William Carter
and
Barbara Hancock

The
Slums

 WASHINGTON SQUARE PRESS · NEW YORK

THE SLUMS

Washington Square Press edition published January, 1970

L

Published by
Washington Square Press, a division of Simon & Schuster, Inc.,
630 Fifth Avenue, New York, N.Y.

WASHINGTON SQUARE PRESS editions are distributed in the
U.S. by Simon & Schuster, Inc., 630 Fifth Avenue, New
York, N.Y. 10020 and in Canada by Simon & Schuster
of Canada, Ltd., Richmond Hill, Ontario, Canada.

1 2 3 4 5 1 0 9

*To my parents
who taught me to live
in urban America*

ACKNOWLEDGMENT

This is one of a series of volumes designed to become text materials for urban schools. Partially funded under Title I, Elementary and Secondary Education Act, Public Law 89–10, 1965, the series grew out of a curriculum development project conceived and executed by the editor. Washington Square Press and the Curriculum Committee of the Trenton, New Jersey, public schools provided valuable editorial assistance.

Mrs. Bernice Munce is Project Supervisor of the Curriculum Committee which includes the following members: William Carter, Elsie Collins, Albert De-Martin, Harold P. DuShane, Barbara Hancock, Roland Hence, Steven McLaine, Gerald Popkin, Richard Scheetz, Carol West.

Also contributing to the effort were Neil O'Donnel, Joseph Fonseca and Eugene Winchester as research assistants, Mrs. Eileen Donohue as secretary, and my wife who spent hours typing and proofreading.

Preface

This book, one volume in a series of introductory studies on problems of American society, is designed to introduce the reader to the dilemma of urban slums, a problem which is of direct and immediate concern to him. Few problems are as explosive or as resistant of solution as is the persistence of slums in the great cities of the world.

A slum may be filled with hope or with despair. The slums of yesterday were essentially filled with hope. Those of today are mainly filled with despair. Where the slums of yesterday seemed way stations on the road to something better in American life, the slums of today are, for too many, permanent homes in which the dramas of life will be played out. These dramas are likely to be tragic, with undertones of bitter comedy designed to make the poignancy of the tragedy even starker.

This book begins with a brief overview of the problems of city slums. It examines some of the reasons why slums persist despite the sometimes heroic efforts made to obliterate them. An introductory essay is followed by a series of fifteen selected readings. The annotations help the reader to identify some of the more difficult terms and concepts, and discussion questions are designed to help him think about one or more problems associated with each reading. It should be emphasized that these readings were chosen with a view toward presenting varied interpretations; as a result, they do not necessarily agree with one another. The disagreement shows that the problem of slums is a thorny one which thus far has resisted efforts to solve it. Have these efforts been inadequate? Can the young in our schools today be prepared in such a way that, as adults, they can contribute to a final solution to that problem? It may be that a significant breakthrough can be made in solving the dilemma of slum housing by encouraging a more complete understanding of the problem itself. It was to help bring about such an understanding that this volume was prepared. We hope that in some small measure, at least, it has realized its goal.

G. L.

Contents

Contents

Part One

The Problem
and the
Challenge

(Sam Falk, Pictorial Parade)

IF you visit the center of any large city in America, you will find that what stand out the most are the lavish homes, mansions, and luxurious apartments of the very rich and the ramshackle hovels of the poor. While it is true that in all cities middle-class housing exists in the form of modest but superior homes and apartments, it is a fact of a city's life today that its outstanding physical characteristic is the sharp contrast between its housing for the rich and that for the poor. Essentially, the dilemma of urban housing is: "If the few can live so well, why is it so difficult to provide at least clean and attractive housing for all?"

Food, clothing, and shelter are the basic necessities of life. The clothes of the poor, as Michael Harrington has pointed out, may have the effect of hiding their poverty.[1] The food of the poor, while more obviously different in quantity and quality from that of the rich, nevertheless does not ordinarily contrast sharply. It is in the area of shelter that differences between the rich and the poor may be seen with the greatest clarity. If these differences are so striking, why has so little been done? Measures taken have been inadequate, even though Jacob Riis vividly portrayed the hovels of the poor as early as the beginning of the twentieth century.

Why has it taken so long for people to act? And why have their actions failed to change the dwelling places of the poor in any considerable way?

What Is a Slum?

The ramshackle houses of the poor are described as slums. But a definition based on descriptions of the houses alone would be misleading. Dilapidated buildings exist, to be sure. But slums are more than broken-down buildings. A slum is where broken-down men and women wage an almost hopeless fight to live decently.

The human damage in the slum may be seen in its high rate of crime and delinquency, as well as in its high rate of infant deaths. The children of the slum drop out of school and thus cut their ties with any hope of self-betterment. Human damage is also reflected in the large numbers of broken families and families with no male breadwinner. Human tragedy is seen every summer morning. When the prosperous, or the moderately prosperous, are on their way to work, the poor are on the stoops of their ruined, broken-down tenements, glad to leave their overheated rooms to catch a breath of the cool early-morning air. There is no way for them to leave their homes. No jobs to go to, no work to do, no duty to perform. A ruined life becomes the product of bricks and mortar that have been allowed to decay too long. A slum is a place where hope is dead.

Who Lives in a Slum?

In every generation, the slum was the home for the newcomer to the city. It was here that the im-

Peeled walls, cracked linoleum, old and ragged furniture—
that's how it is in the homes of the poor. (Joe Molnar)

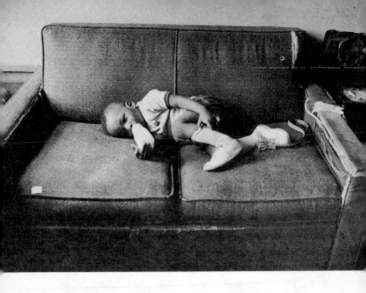

(Joe Molnar)

migrant found himself when he left his ship. It was here, among friends and relatives, that he stayed and lived until he got a job. The Italians, the Irish, the Jews, the Russians, the Scandinavians all, at one time or another, lived in the worst housing of the big cities—its slums. The newcomers who lived there had a number of characteristics in common. For one thing, they were poor and could afford no better housing. They crowded into existing apartments with friends and relatives, sometimes sharing the rent, sometimes requiring and accepting charity. In addition, they all wanted and indeed needed to be with other recent immigrants who could help them get a new start in life. Here they could speak their own language and follow their own customs while learning new ones. They also came to the slums because they had to be near the central business district in order to work or look for work. To live farther out would have required carfare, and that was a luxury they could ill afford.

The slum is the dwelling place of the minority. This was as true 50 years ago as it is today. But the minorities have changed. Today, the Negro is the minority group one most often associates with the slums. While there are many fine black neighborhoods, for the most part the Negro has taken the place of former immigrants as the most common resident of the slums. In the slums of the major cities, Puerto Ricans may also be found in relatively large numbers, but since there are fewer of them in the total population, their concentration is not as great as that of the Negro. Other, perhaps more exotic minorities make up the slums of some American cities. The Chinatown of San Francisco is in part a slum. There is a Navajo slum in St. Louis, a Chippewa slum in Minneapolis. The Kenmore district of Chicago is unique in that it is made up of white, Protestant Americans from the rural areas of Appalachia. The hillbillies, although native-born and white, are nevertheless new to the city, and their poverty makes them eligible for the slum.[2]

Whether he is Negro, Puerto Rican, Mexican, Chippewa, or hillbilly, today's slum dweller is not so much new to America as new to the city. Many of the immigrants of former generations came from the teeming cities or rural villages of Europe. Although they were desperately poor, they learned what city life was like. Today's newcomer is a stranger to city life. He comes from a shack on a rural farm, and the city bewilders him. He is frequently unable to read and write and may lack the skills required to get a job in the city. Often he lacks the essential knowledge needed to keep a room clean

In the slums black and white alike experience a mutual feeling of rejection, and in their need to survive there is little time to ponder tomorrow. (OEO)

or get rid of garbage, and sometimes even the knowledge he needs to use water and toilet facilities that are provided.

Most of today's slum dwellers find learning to live in the city more difficult than former groups did. The schools do not seem to provide the tools of reading and writing as effectively as they did for the former immigrant. Jobs are more difficult to obtain and income improves little, if at all. The slum, which was a point of departure for the previous inhabitants, is now a jail. Poverty and prejudice are the twins that tie people to the ghetto, seemingly forever.

Where Are the Slums?

In a real sense slums are everywhere. No city is without them. Even in the country, the shacks of migrant farm workers and sharecroppers may be regarded as slums. Slums may be found in the large industrial centers of any nation, in Manchester, England, as well as Pittsburgh, Pennsylvania. They may be found in the swamplands of India or in Puerto Rico; in the cliff-like dwellings of Naples, Italy, or in the old caves of southern Spain.

The slums that concern us here, however, are the ones that exist in the large cities of America. The same cities that have produced our highest forms of culture have subjected huge numbers of people to the lowest form of urban life. That slums should exist in Calcutta, Hong Kong, or Istanbul comes as no surprise. These are old cities that have failed over the centuries to keep up with the housing needs of their people. But the cities of America, by comparison, are new. Yet they too, over a much shorter period of time, have failed to keep up with the need of the people for good homes or apartments in which to live.

Rarely has a large city been without a slum. But in every city the location and nature of the slum has changed from generation to generation. In the past, most slums were limited to a crowded section in the old center of the city. The rich lived nearby or in suburbs. While they were often in close proximity to the slum, the well-to-do found it possible and often convenient to ignore its presence. The slum seemed stationary, with fixed and unchanging boundaries. Since it was not growing, there was little to worry about. Or at least this seemed to be true.

Unemployment Rates: Ghetto Areas and Surrounding Metropolitan Areas

SMSA *	GHETTO AREA	Unemployment rate GHETTO **	SMSA †
Boston	Roxbury	6.9	3.7
Cleveland	Hough and surrounding neighborhood	15.6	3.5
Detroit	Central Woodward	10.1	4.3
Los Angeles	South Los Angeles	12.0	6.0
New York	Harlem	8.1	4.6
	East Harlem	9.0	
	Bedford-Stuyvesant	6.2	
Philadelphia	North Philadelphia	11.0	4.3
Phoenix	Salt River Bed	13.2	—
St. Louis	North Side	12.9	4.5
San Antonio	East and West Sides	8.1	—
San Francisco-Oakland	Mission-Fillmore	11.1	5.2
	Bayside	13.0	

* Standard Metropolitan Statistical Area
** as of November 1966
† average for year ending August 1966

SOURCE: 1967 Manpower Report of the President, page 75; metropolitan area data are based on special tabulation of data from the Current Population Survey.

A comparison of unemployment in ghetto areas with unemployment in metropolitan areas as a whole during 1966 shows the ghetto rate to be approximately two to four times the rate in metropolitan areas.

Lion In The Streets

© 1967 Herblock, The Washington Post

Today, however, the slum is different. It grows and spreads out just as the city does. The slum areas now seem to surround the business district and reach out into the suburbs as well. The slum of today is less compact than it once was and covers more land. Often it is not even in a very old neighborhood. Instead, it may be in a neighborhood that was occupied first by the rich and then by the middle class. One such example is New York's Harlem. First the area contained the luxurious homes of the rich. Later, it became a bit more crowded, with middle-class Jews, Italians, Irish, and Germans moving in. Starting in 1910, Harlem slowly began to change again as black migrants from the South started to arrive in search of jobs and opportunity. When they failed in their search, "Harlem became a prison of its new residents."[3] As more and more blacks came, they too settled in Harlem and it became overcrowded; in addition, it lacked many of the essential services a community must have if its people are to live in dignity. Thus, in three generations, or in about 60 years, this once-rich section of New York became the "Dark Ghetto" of today and one of the largest slums in the nation.

Why Do Slums Grow?

Despite heroic efforts to end slums, urban blight is spreading. Like a disease, slums seem to grow and multiply. A distinguished student of urban affairs writes:

> Hover [in a helicopter] motionless over America's major cities and you will shortly be impressed by two facts: As a rule, only minute portions of the older areas of our cities have so far been subjected to rebuilding and renewal. . . . Second, the areas of the city which have been the subject of the most intensive renewal activity tend to be in or near the city's central business district.[4]

The author goes on to point out that in a city like New York, which has a long history of battles against the slums, less than three square miles of the surface of the city has been improved.[5]

It has been estimated that ". . . one out of every four families lives in homes that are inadequate, deteriorating, and that are the seedbeds of slum areas."[6] Probably more than one in every seven urban families live in dwelling units unfit for human habitation.[7]

Despite some occasional heroic efforts, America seems unable to keep the disease of slums from spreading. It infects relatively healthy portions of the city and feeds upon itself like a cancer. Those who can afford it move out of the central city. Newcomers move in, often doubling up to save costs. Single rooms become available for rent. Small business enterprises such as barber shops, beauty parlors, and vegetable stands enter the area. If the country is going through a depression, as it did in the 1930's, less money is spent on the services people need. The streets fall into disrepair. Garbage accumulates because collections are slow. Buildings become even more run-down. Those who live in the slums require more help, but less is available. Worse, absentee landlords prey on slum dwellers. They make few repairs and encourage overcrowding and the sharing of bathrooms and kitchens. Often they give little heat or hot water. Since taxes and expenses are low, their profits are high. Even if they are at last brought into court for breaking the law and are made to pay fines, they merely add these to the "cost of doing business in the slum," and continue to profit from the misery of the people.

No city can be proud of its slums. Not only are they ugly to look at, but they are costly as well. Two types of costs are characteristic of slums. The first of these may be thought of as social costs, and

An avenue of despair. This alleyway cluttered with waste and debris is one of thousands scattered across the nation. (Joe Molnar)

the second as dollar costs. Obviously, the two are closely related, and in many ways they cannot be separated. Nevertheless, we will try to separate them here in order to show clearly the ways in which slums are a costly burden on any city.

What Are the Social Costs of Slums?

The social costs of slums include a high incidence of poverty, ill health, delinquency, and crime. Whether these are causes or results of slum living is not clear. Obviously, the poor live in slums. But also, the slums of today make and keep men poor. Some slums have been described as "slums of hope," others as "slums of despair."[8] The slums of hope are those in which the inhabitants have reason to believe that in time they will leave, or that their children will be able to leave. The slums of despair are those in which the people have given up hope of ever leaving. It is the latter type of slum that creates deep social problems for the city.

Crime and delinquency are associated with slums. But it is still not clear whether slums cause crime, or whether criminals, delinquents, and problem families are attracted to slums. There is reason to believe that in a slum of despair, crime and juvenile delinquency are responses the people have made to their hopelessness. If they cannot "make it" honestly, there appears to be little to lose if they try other ways. A disturbing element in this picture is the fact that many criminal activities that are associated with the slums are encouraged by people living outside the slum who come there to gamble or to buy narcotics. Thus gambling and the illegal sale of drugs, while associated with slums, are also "services" demanded by outsiders.

In a depressed area even Sunday is grim for the people who live there. (Joe Molnar)

Children from the slums often do not do as well in school as other children. They achieve less, and their reading and arithmetic are poor. In a slum of despair, they bring a feeling of hopelessness to school with them. As a result, they see little value in school, and less purpose in going. Lack of schooling in turn contributes to the likelihood that they will never leave the slum. Children of the slums also

go to school irregularly because they are frequently ill. Influenza and pneumonia cause death more frequently than they do in other areas of the city. Infant mortality likewise is high.

Contributing to the failure of children to do well in school is the high level of anxiety that forms the pattern of their lives. Not only are the homes and neighborhoods in which they live crime-infested, but

crisis is a way of life in the family itself. With unemployment a constant threat, hunger and even
eviction from the apartment are always a danger.
Lack of privacy causes friction between husbands
and wives, among children, and between one family
and another. Since many slum families receive welfare payments, privacy is further invaded by the
social worker who must make a monthly investigation to determine if the family is still entitled to assistance.

Finally, and in some ways most important, bad
housing affects the way poor people feel about
themselves and the way other people feel about
them. It's hard to have self-respect in a rat-infested,
crumbling, crowded apartment. When someone
leaves a place like that to try to get a job, he
already feels licked. Similarly, other people think
of poor people in the same terms. Some of them
mistakenly think that poor people are no good
because they live in slums or because the streets
are dirty. Of course, *they've* never lived in a place
where the landlord didn't turn on the heat or where
the city didn't collect the garbage. But, they still
feel that way, and their attitude represents an
important effect of bad housing on poor people.[9]

What Are the Dollar Costs of Slums?

The cost of a slum is a burden upon all the tax-
payers. For one thing, the chief source of revenue
for a city is its real estate. The better the property,
the more it can be taxed. Slums obviously represent
worn-out, run-down property. Because the buildings
have deteriorated, they are less valuable. The result
is that taxes on such property decline. Buildings

that once brought the city a large amount of income no longer do so. The lost income must be made up by higher taxes on other property throughout the city.

Making matters worse is the fact that slums require more, not fewer services. They require more garbage collection and more police, fire, and health protection, not less. These services must be provided, and they must be paid for. Since the people living in the slums cannot pay for them, the people living outside must. "For every dollar needed to service the area [slum], only ten cents [comes] from the area itself."[10] As the burden of taxes falls increasingly on middle-class residents, resentment among them mounts and they move away. As they move and sell their homes to the less prosperous, the cycle of developing slums is encouraged to begin again. Taxes go up and are borne by a smaller and smaller group who must pay for the services needed by the larger and larger slum area.

When an area is prosperous and well serviced by the city, businessmen are encouraged to invest their money there. They open stores or buy real estate. Large chain stores and banks move to the area and it becomes a busy and profitable commercial and shopping center. However, when a slum begins to develop, businessmen become cautious. Chain stores and banks look elsewhere for opportunities to invest. Buildings are sold to "slumlords" who hope to profit by low expenses and overcrowded apartments. Corporations that might have wished to invest their money in new apartment houses or office buildings do not, while industries seek locations outside the central city. When this happens, another source of revenue for the city is lost.

Those stores that remain in the slums begin to

The best way for a slumlord to realize a high profit from his buildings is to turn a deaf ear to the legitimate complaints of his tenants. (Joe Molnar)

economize and put off making needed repairs. In this way they contribute to the ever growing deterioration. Unscrupulous merchants, taking advantage of the poor, charge higher prices here than elsewhere. Because there are few chain stores in such areas, small stores are almost the only ones left to serve the poor. The absence of competition helps raise the prices the poor pay for food, clothing, and other necessities still further, until they are unreasonably high.

It is clear that in terms of money alone, slum clearance makes sense. It is expensive, but it is more expensive when cities do not clear their slums. The cost of slum clearance may be regarded as an investment. It is an investment in human life and hope for those who live in the slums, and it is an investment for the rest of the population, which will prosper only if industry can be encouraged to remain in the city rather than run away. Slum clearance has been said to be the only way in which cities can help themselves. It is probably the key to the tiresome list of urban problems cities face. The two chief ways in which cities, with Federal help, have sought to clear the slums are through public housing and urban renewal.

What Are Public Housing and Urban Renewal?

Public housing may be defined as the construction of low-rent apartments by the city, state, or Federal government. Public housing is paid for by government funds and is both built and managed by a government agency. In the United States, the provision of adequate housing has mainly been the responsibility of the city and state. The interest of cities and states in housing varies widely. Some do little or nothing at all, while others do a great deal. New York City may be regarded as one that has tried to do a great deal. As early as 1867, it passed a law preventing the building of rooms without windows, and, in 1901, provision was made to improve facilities for sanitation, air, light, and fire protection.

However, it was not until the depression of the 1930's that cities and states fully awoke to the deterioration that had taken place despite the laws that had been passed to prevent it. It was about this time that the Federal government began to play a significant role in providing adequate housing for the people. In 1934, under the New Deal program 'of Franklin D. Roosevelt, the Federal Housing Administration was created. Its purpose was to encourage the purchase and repair of homes by making it possible to borrow money at low rates of interest. In 1934, the United States encouraged the development of public housing by passing the National Housing Act, which was designed to encourage improved housing for the poor. The United States Housing Authority was also established (1937). It had the power to grant low-interest loans to cities that agreed to clear slums and build low-rent public housing projects. The purpose of Federal action in providing public housing was to help the country out of a depression by helping the building industry. It was hoped that in this way other industries also would be helped, that jobs would increase and with them the purchasing power of the consumer. Above all, it was felt that this belated start in the field of public housing would help to eliminate slums.

In 1949, the Federal government took a major step in slum clearance by granting building funds

New low-income apartments in Roxbury, Massachusetts.
(Norman Gordon)

to cities that agreed to buy land in slum areas and
then sell the land at a loss to private builders, who
in turn would agree to build new, low-cost housing
on it. Most of the loss would be borne by the Federal government, and the rest by the city. Urban
renewal and public housing are similar in that both
attempt to rid cities of slums and provide the poor
with better homes. But where public housing essentially is concerned with individual buildings or
projects, urban renewal involves large-scale planning, such as the destruction of many blocks of
slums in the center of a city and the replacement of
these slums with better apartments for the poor. Included in urban renewal projects are efforts to plan
for future city growth. Traffic and transit problems
and the cultural rebirth of the center of the city
are also among the goals of urban renewal. With the
start of urban renewal, it was expected that the

As part of its urban renewal program, Trenton, New Jersey, plans to replace this deteriorated housing. (Trenton Times Library)

slums would come tumbling down with the speed of the walls of Jericho. However, this did not happen.

Because slum clearance was not proceeding rapidly enough and because the problems of the cities seemed to be growing, in 1965 the Congress of the United States created the Department of Housing and Urban Development. Robert C. Weaver was appointed Secretary of the Department and, as such, became the first Negro to serve in the Cabinet of a U.S. President. His job was to coordinate the efforts made by the Federal government in encouraging slum clearance. The Federal Housing Administration and the U.S. Housing Authority were incorporated into this department, which also is largely responsible for the government's urban renewal programs.

What Have Public Housing and Urban Renewal Accomplished?

The goal of public housing and urban renewal has been to give every family in the United States decent housing. This goal has not been met. Much remains to be done, but much has been accomplished. The full story of what has been done would be too long to tell here. But in Los Angeles, 10,000 new low-rent housing units have been built. St. Louis' slum clearance programs have brought new beauty to that city. Philadelphia, Pittsburgh, Trenton, and Chicago have all undertaken vast slum clearance projects, and New York's Lincoln Center and Pittsburgh's Golden Triangle were made possible through Federal urban renewal funds.

Most large cities have undertaken urban renewal projects. These projects not only try to replace slums, but also seek to attack the social and economic problems that are usually found there. Thus, urban renewal encourages cultural growth and community participation. It improves school buildings, provides local leadership, fights crime and delinquency, and seeks to provide open areas for rest, play, and relaxation. In Philadelphia, an effort was made to encourage the men of skid row to give up whisky and regain a respectable place in society. "We are on the way," wrote Robert C. Weaver, former Secretary of Housing and Urban Development; ". . . we shall not only improve the program but also forge the instruments for dealing more effectively with some of the human problems which have been ignored and avoided."[11]

Where Have Public Housing and Urban Renewal Failed?

Although public housing and urban renewal have achieved a measure of success, they also have been severely criticized. For one thing, there are people who believe that government construction of homes and apartments violates the spirit of free enterprise. Builders often maintain that, as a result of what they regard as government interference, costs are unnecessarily high and opportunities for profit unnecessarily limited. While the building industry may complain, it is clear, nevertheless, that the slums could not be cleared by relying upon free enterprise alone.

There are other, perhaps more serious problems associated with urban renewal that require recognition. These may be summarized as follows:

1. In the nearly 20 years since urban renewal has been a reality, the slums have endured. While

much has been done, too much still remains to be accomplished. In short, urban renewal and public housing, in the view of some, have not renewed large enough areas of the run-down sections of the central cities.

2. Part of the reason may be found in the relatively small sums spent on public housing and urban renewal. These are especially small compared with the sums spent on war or highways. When it comes to public housing, "Congressmen think small."[12]

3. In both public housing and urban renewal there is such a vast amount of "red tape" that it has made some cities unwilling to apply for Federal assistance. In urban renewal programs, it takes many years from the date of initial application by a city to the completion of construction by the builders.

4. It must be remembered that, while the city and the Federal government agree to buy urban renewal property below cost and share the loss, private developers must do the building. These developers want to anticipate a profit before undertaking the effort; however, this is not always possible without huge outlays of funds. Moreover, because of the length of time it takes to make application, buy up slums, and build, profits are often long delayed.

5. Although it attempts to improve living conditions for those in the slums, urban renewal often subjects them to the hardship of relocation. Families must be moved and new apartments found that will not cost more than the old ones. As a result, tenants from one slum are likely to become tenants of another. The long-range planning that must take place may demoralize the residents. This is particularly true if there is uncertainty as to whether or not the area in which they live actually will be re-

"I'D SETTLE FOR SOME <u>CLOSED</u> HOUSING."

(Pat Fink)

built. In the meantime, landlords often let their property run down even more.

6. Making matters worse is the fact that those who are relocated have little or no assurance that they can get into one of the shiny new apartments. For one thing, since the slums are overcrowded, the new apartments obviously cannot house the same number of people as the old ones did. When a fair amount of the space is allocated to each tenant, fewer families can be accommodated. The remainder stay in the slums.

7. The brand-new apartments to which slum tenants look forward may cost too much in the long run. Private developers may be faced with higher costs, so that they must raise rents to make a fair profit. These rents are higher than those the tenants of the slums paid before. It has been one of the criticisms of urban renewal that the poor are moved out and the middle class is moved in.

8. Public housing projects are usually gigantic apartment buildings. These buildings, new and clean (at least in the beginning), have been described as ". . . cold, impersonal, cheerless . . ."[13] places in which to live. There are too many rules for tenant behavior, and too much discipline is exercised by the project manager. The project is run like an institution, not a residence.[14]

9. In order to be eligible to live in a low-rent housing project, one must have a low income. As soon as income rises beyond a certain limit, the tenant must move to private housing. Often, while his income is too high for public housing, it is too low for comparable private housing. Such a tenant may be forced to move back into a slum.

10. Adding to the problems of public housing and urban renewal is the presence of racial prej-

udice and discrimination in housing. The inhabitants of today's slums in the central cities include large numbers of Negroes and Puerto Ricans. Urban renewal and public housing have been charged with failure to achieve integrated and adequate housing for all. How to provide fair housing for all, regardless of race, is another of the grave dilemmas of urban housing.

How Does Discrimination Aggravate the Urban Housing Problem?

It has been said that housing is the one thing ". . . in the American market that is not freely available on equal terms to anyone who can afford to pay."[15] If low income doesn't keep the Negro in the slums, white prejudice against him does. If some blacks break out and move into white neighborhoods, it is not long before whites begin to run away. The faster they run, the faster a new ghetto is created.

The creation of the Negro ghetto in the Bedford-Stuyvesant district of Brooklyn is an illustration. Before the 1930's, the neighborhood consisted of the large homes of the relatively wealthy. When the depression came in 1929, many owners found that they could no longer maintain their homes; the cost of running them was too high, they were unable to pay for servants, and taxes were increasing. At this point the technique known as "block-busting" was initiated by some real estate salesmen. Block-busting consists of getting a single Negro family into a house in a formerly all-white neighborhood. The real estate operator then contacts all the other white homeowners in the area and offers to buy their homes because "the neighborhood is changing."

Fear that the changed neighborhood will force a drop in the values of their homes causes the whites to panic and sell to the real estate operator at a low price. The real estate firm then finds other Negro families to whom it sells the houses at high profits. The black families pay the higher price because they have less choice and cannot "shop around" to find something equally good for less money. This block-busting technique, used in the 1930's, launched the Bedford-Stuyvesant ghetto of today.

Not only is a great deal of housing closed to Negroes because whites will not rent them apartments (even when they can pay the rent) or sell them houses (even when they can pay the price), but Negroes trying to find adequate housing have encountered other problems as well. For example, they have found that, compared to whites, they have to pay more for the same or similar apartments or houses. Moreover, when they try to buy a house, they often are forced to pay higher mortgage interest rates than whites do. In short, "the dollar in the dark hand does not have the same purchasing power as the dollar in the white hand."[16] In most places, discriminatory practices are against the law. But enforcing the law is difficult and housing segregation remains a major problem of the great cities of America.

Failure to integrate housing may be taken as a yardstick by which to measure our lack of progress toward achieving an integrated society in America. Segregated housing means segregated schooling. The Supreme Court decision of 1954 ordering an end to segregated schools has not yet been obeyed, largely because housing patterns in the North as well as those in the South remain segregated. Deteriorated, segregated slum housing contributes to failure in

The Reverend James Groppi, advisor of Milwaukee's NAACP Youth Council and active demonstrator for open housing, has had to buck local regulations prohibiting demonstrations at night. (UPI)

school, to ill health, and to unemployment. It spins its own web of failure and despair.

How May Open Housing Be Achieved?

By "open housing" we mean a policy that makes homes and apartments equally available to all, without regard to race or color. Until 1948, government policy in housing encouraged residential segregation.

Houses were sold with agreements between the seller and the buyer that the buyer would neither sell nor rent to Negroes. Often such agreements were made against Jews as well. In 1948, however, the United States Supreme Court held that these agreements violated the Constitution and were illegal. Nevertheless, this decision did little to further housing integration, since violations of the decision could not be easily punished.

The trend since 1948 has been to end Federally supported segregated housing. This policy was given an important boost on November 20, 1962, when President Kennedy, by Executive Order, barred discrimination in all housing that received Federal aid. This meant that all housing operated by the government, such as the homes built for families of soldiers, would be open to all. It meant further that any housing built with the help of a Federal loan, or any urban renewal project, would also be open to all. This Executive Order was incorporated into the Civil Rights Act two years later. While the Executive Order and the Civil Rights Act were steps in the right direction, they applied primarily to new housing. Old housing remained segregated.

As has been pointed out, regulation of housing has been largely the responsibility of the states and the cities. The President's Executive Order had the effect of encouraging states and cities to move more rapidly toward "open" housing for all. Many states and many of the large cities of the country have since done so. States like New York, New Jersey, Pennsylvania, Massachusetts, and Michigan have laws that go farther in bringing about free choice in housing , and in some cities, block-busting methods by real estate operators have been forbidden.

Despite the law and despite good intentions, segregated housing remains a fact of city life. For one thing, city, state, and Federal laws against discrimination in housing are difficult to enforce. It takes more than law to change the habits and attitudes built up in a century of housing discrimination. Also, the practices of some government housing agencies seem to have the effect of encouraging segregation, although this is not done deliberately. But in granting housing loans to veterans and others, credit standards are used that seem to qualify many more whites than Negroes.

It is obvious that open housing has not yet been achieved. It is equally obvious that integration of society and elimination of the slums, as well as elimination of the crime, delinquency, ill health, and inferior education that are all associated with the slums, essentially depend on open housing. The achievement of open housing is also dependent on the Negro's level of employment and living standards. As these improve, he will be able to exercise his economic power to buy a house or rent an apartment wherever he wishes.

Is the Model Cities Program the Answer to Slum Housing?

In 1967, Congress passed the "model cities" program. Sixty-three cities were said to be eligible to receive Federal funds for the purpose of building model cities. The model cities program recognizes the fact that problems of slum housing are intimately related to problems of local government, city planning, poverty, unemployment, ill health, and inferior education. It suggests that merely rebuilding houses is no longer enough. Instead, a whole city, or at least a large part of its run-down sections, must be rehabilitated, not only to provide better housing, but also to improve the total welfare of the people of the community.

The National Housing Act of 1934 was an attempt to provide better housing by tearing down slum buildings and putting up housing projects. Urban renewal was a program of slum clearance extending over a number of blocks. The model cities program appears to be a further extension of the attack on slums which deals with the problem in nearly all its aspects. While it is unlikely that there will be enough funds to rebuild an entire city, dramatic improvements are possible if cities use their money to plan for entire neighborhoods. An important part of such overall neighborhood planning includes work with the people of the neighborhood themselves.

It is too soon to say whether or not the model cities program is the way to eliminate slums. But since the slums grow out of a great variety of problems, it seems appropriate to attack them on many fronts, not just one. The model cities program may change the slums of despair into slums of hope. While it is more than likely that the older generation living in the slums today will end their lives there, there is reason to believe that the younger generation, through the combined efforts of the people themselves and the city, state, and Federal governments, will find their way to better housing.

Part Two.

Selected
Readings

Jacob August Riis, author and social reformer, was born in Denmark in 1849 and came to America in 1870. In 1877 he joined the staff of the "New York Tribune"; later he worked on the "New York Sun." As a reporter, Riis pointed out the evils of urban life. Actively campaigning to improve conditions in the slums, he pioneered tenement house reform and helped build playgrounds and small parks. The book from which this is taken was published in 1890.

1

How the Other Half Lives

by JACOB A. RIIS

BOTTLE Alley is around the corner in Baxter Street; but it is a fair specimen of its kind, wherever found. Look into any of these houses: everywhere the same pile of rags, of malodorous bones and musty paper, all of which the sanitary police flatter themselves they have banished to the

From *How the Other Half Lives* by Jacob A. Riis, American Century Series edition (New York: Hill and Wang, 1962), pp. 48–49. Copyright © 1957 by Hill and Wang, Inc.

Bottle Alley, Mulberry Ben. (Photograph by Jacob A. Riis; the Jacob A. Riis Collection, Museum of the City of New York)

dumps and warehouses. Here is a "flat" or "parlor" and two pitch dark coops called bedrooms. Truly, the bed is all there is room for. The family tea kettle is on the stove, doing duty for the time being as a wash-boiler. By night it will have returned to its proper use again, a practical illustration of how poverty in "The Bend" makes both ends meet. One, two, three beds are there, if the old boxes and heaps of foul straw can be called by that name; a broken stove with a crazy pipe from which the smoke leaks at every joint, a table of rough boards propped up on boxes, piles of rubbish in the corner. The close-

Baxter Street Alley. (Photograph by Jacob A. Riis; the Jacob A. Riis Collection, Museum of the City of New York)

ness and smell are appalling. How many people sleep here? The woman with the red bandana shakes her head sullenly, but the bare-legged girl with the bright face counts on her fingers—five, six! "Six, sir." Six grown people and five children. "Only five," she says with a smile, swathing the little one on her lap in its cruel bandage. There is another in the cradle—actually a cradle. And how much the rent?

Nine and a half,* and "please sir! he won't put the paper on." "He" is the landlord. The "paper" hangs in musty shreds on the wall. Well do I recollect the visit of a health inspector to one of these tenements on a July day when the thermometer outside was climbing high in the nineties; but inside, in that awful room, with half a dozen persons washing, cooking, and sorting rags, lay the dying baby alongside the stove, where the doctor's thermometer ran up to 115°! Perishing for the want of a breath of air in this city of untold charities! Did not the manager of the Fresh Air Fund write to the pastor of an Italian church only last year that "no one asked for Italian children," and hence he could not send any to the country?

FURTHER INQUIRY

1. To what extent do the slum conditions of 1890 exist today?
2. Why do slums still exist in every large city of the nation?
3. How effective were the writings of Jacob Riis in bringing about social reform?
4. How did Riis use photography to illustrate the squalid conditions in which many Americans of his day lived? (See the original publication as well.)

Nine and a half—$9.50 per month.

In this selection, the author writes about the high hopes that were held for the building at 311 East 100th Street when it was built more than 60 years ago. In its day the plans for the new building marked a great improvement in living quarters for the poor. Who is more responsible for seeing to it that the hopes for a building are realized, the tenants or the owners?

2

A House of Hope

by WOODY KLEIN

AND on that spring morning (April 19, 1906), thirty-three hopeful New York families moved into the freshly painted apartments of 311 East 100th Street.

The building at number 311 had actually been conceived nineteen months earlier when a new-building application, Plan No. 400, had been filed by the owners, Louis Meryash, of 96 Monroe Street, and Albert London, of 263 Broome Street, at the city Tenement House Department's Manhattan office, 61 Irving Place, on October 5, 1904.

The application for the erection of the new brick

From *Let In the Sun* by Woody Klein (New York: Macmillan, 1964), pp. 60–62, 73–75. Copyright © 1964 by Woody Klein. Reprinted with permission of The Macmillan Company.

The house at 311 East 100th Street. (Phil Stanziola)

tenement house specified it would contain fire escapes opening directly from at least one room in each apartment; a brick bulkhead in the roof with stairs leading to it; iron risers and banisters; steel beams throughout the structure; ceilings of angle irons and terra-cotta blocks; metal-covered door, window, and stair trims; all doors self-closing and fire-proofed; all shafts fire-proofed.

Each room, according to the application, would have at least one window opening directly on the street or yard, each water closet* would have small windows, each public hall and stair hall would have at least one window opening on the street. The cellar would be made damp-proof by means of asphalt, and lighted and ventilated by means of windows and glass doors opening upon the courts and yards. All courts, vent shafts, areas, and yards would be properly graded with cement and drained and connected with the street sewer. Gas was to be the source of light and heat. Sinks would be installed in each apartment and supplied with running water from a roof tank holding 2,500 gallons.

The application was signed by the owners' architectural firm, Horenburger and Straus, of 122 Bowery, and it specified that number 311 would be erected as one of five adjacent tenement houses. The first of the buildings was to be built on the north side of East 100th Street, 100 feet east of Second Avenue on a lot 40 feet by 100 feet eleven inches. The building at 311 was the third building to be erected in the row on what was designated as Lot No. 9 of city block No. 1672. The owners-builders estimated the cost of each building, exclusive of the lot, to be $40,000.

.   .   .

On April 19, 1906, the house at 311 East 100th Street was completed. The property, which had changed hands seven times since London and Meryash filed plans for it in 1904, was now owned by a couple named Hyman and Rose Levin. The Mitral Realty and Construction Company had just put the final touches on the building and it was, at last,

---

water closet—toilet.

ready to take its place among the fine new-law*
tenements on the emerging East 100th Street block.

Rents in the clean new structure averaged about
$15 an apartment, rather high for tenement rentals.
The rents in this eastern section of Harlem were
higher, too, than those in the Lower East Side,
where the poorer families still lived. So desirable
were the apartments in number 311 and the other
new-law buildings on the block that nearly half
the families who moved in paid 20 to 30 per cent
of their monthly income for rent.

In this young neighborhood the new-law tenements were occupied mostly by Jewish families who
had moved from the Lower East Side. Nearly 50
per cent of these families had breadwinners who
earned their living through skilled, manual, or
mechanical labor; less than 20 per cent performed
unskilled labor; and the remaining 30 per cent
worked at clerical or trade jobs or in the profes-
sions.

Nearly half the immigrants to the rapidly growing
East Harlem area came directly from the depths of
the Lower East Side in the hope of starting anew
in a fresher and safer atmosphere. About one-third
of the newcomers came from the nearby neighborhood and fewer than 10 per cent came directly
from Europe.

They came for better-quality homes, to improve
their social status, to be in more pleasant surroundings, and to give their children everything they did
not have themselves. They came not so much because they were crowded out of the older districts of
Manhattan as because they were young, enterpris-

---

new-law—this term refers to buildings which were put
up according to the latest building code of 1901.

ing, and in search of better conditions. They wanted to find roots in a new community which had both the assets and the hopes of a new-born neighborhood on the threshold of a new life.

As the tenants moved into number 311 on that warm spring day in 1906, life around them held out real hope. The Union Settlement House nearby exerted a desirable influence and the City of New York itself had just completed two recreation centers near local public schools and had added a branch to the public library.

And so, with a flamboyant page of New York City's housing history immediately behind it, the house on East 100th Street opened at a time when the institution of the new-law tenements seemed to be the greatest innovation of the dawning Twentieth Century.

The new-law tenement, symbolized by 311 East 100th Street, was held up as the solution to the city's housing problems. It was the building that would forever mark the end of slums in New York City. It was the house of hope.

FURTHER INQUIRY

1. Were the high hopes held for this building justified? Why or why not?
2. What was new about the application to build at the site of 311 in 1904?
3. Why were the new-law tenements regarded as "the greatest innovation of the dawning Twentieth Century"?

Here the author describes how the building at 311 East 100th Street, which was built to be a "house of hope," came to be a "house of horror." In this selection he writes about one of the families in the building. Do the people living here deserve our sympathy? Do the owners deserve our blame? Why or why not?

3

A House of Horrors

by WOODY KLEIN

THIRTY-THREE families occupy the house at 311 East 100th Street. A total of 139 people live in seventy-two rooms, excluding kitchens and bathrooms. Family sizes range from single people to two adults and eight children. The average adult age is forty-two. The average length of stay in the house is 6.3 years. The oldest tenant has been in the house for twenty years.

The adults and teen-age children have had an average of six years of schooling. Family incomes average about $60 per week, or about $3,100 per

From *Let In the Sun* by Woody Klein (New York: Macmillan, 1964), pp. 21–25. Copyright © 1964 by Woody Klein. Reprinted with permission of The Macmillan Company.

"I live here because I can't move."—Mrs. Petra Rodriguez.
(Phil Stanziola)

year. The highest income is $110 per week in one
family where the husband and wife are both working. The lowest is $10 per week, a death benefit for
a woman from the British West Indies.

The working men and women hold jobs which include delivery man, porter, dressmaker, houseclean-
er, laborer, mechanic, desk installer, power press
operator, laundry worker, hospital worker, machin-
ist, food-store helper, garment worker, construction
worker, and superintendent.

To understand the tragedy of the house at number
311—the human suffering which goes far deeper
than the physical neglect of the building—we must
look at more than statistics and the vague shadows
of people packed layer over layer in this tenement.
We must study their faces and listen to their hopes,
fears, and ordinary thoughts.

Marcellino Rodriguez, a forty-nine-year-old native
of Rio Piedras, Puerto Rico, came to the United
States in 1957 and worked as superintendent of the
house at number 311. On his sad, cinnamon-col-
ored face is an expression of bewilderment and
weariness.

"In Rio Piedras I work as a cabinetmaker, a
carpenter," he tells you in broken English. "But I
need more money for my family. Salary no good
there. Carpenter make about twenty-five to thirty
dollars a week there. So I come here. But here I
no gotta union card so I take other jobs. When I
first came here I lived in Cherry Street downtown.
I like it better there."

Rodriguez is the father of twelve children, including four adopted from his wife's first marriage. His
oldest child is his twenty-four-year-old son, Marcellino, Jr., who quit high school after his junior
year to take a job as a grocery clerk, moved next

door to his parents and family in number 311. Rodriguez' other children range in age from two to twenty-two. It is a handsome family with five robust boys and seven pretty girls.

Unable to acquire a membership card in the carpenter's union, Rodriguez finally found an apartment and a job in 311 East 100th Street. He took on the task of superintendent of the building in 1960 and relinquished it in 1963 when, disgusted and depressed by his financial problems, he gave up everything and fled to a nearby New Jersey town one day to get away from his home. Before he left his family and his job, however, he had learned enough about the maintenance operations of the building to complain:

"Too much work. I have three rooms and twelve in the family. My family has no room. The money is no good. I was on welfare but they close my case because when an investigator came to my house he argued too much with my wife. Too much trouble with my family. I had to take my big children out of school because I got no money to buy them clothes. I got no money for one dollar fifty a day for lunch. My one son doesn't go to work or to school because he has no clothes, carfare, or money. Once I make hundred dollars a week in New Jersey as a carpenter when I first come here, but now they got no more work for me. I need more money for my family. The money I win now is no good for my family."

Does he like where he is living?

Rodriguez pauses, his blue eyes forlornly expressing his feeling of hopelessness.

"No, I no like it here," he says slowly. "I don't like this area because too much drunk, too many, I see people too much drunk. . . . I want to have a house for my family . . . when my family gets sick we have no room here. . . . I send them to hospital. I have no refrigerator. Day by day good food in my house spoil because I got no money to buy refrigerator. I asked the landlord for one. He says he can no give me one. I said to him about the electric light. He says same. He says I must fix it myself. He no want to take care of it. He says it is my business. The whole building is no good. The halls no good. The door out front no good. No glass in the door. The mailboxes no good. The boiler no good. I work all day there. I live in the boiler. I put coal in the boiler, too much. He no fix nothing. He pays me hundred twelve dollars a month, that's all."

How are the other tenants in the house?

"Regular, regular," he replies with a faint smile. "Some are no good. Bad people. Poor. I get off my bed at four o'clock in the morning. I don't go to bed at night until eleven o'clock. I work all the hours. I get up and go to hallway. I take broom and sweep the stairs in the house. I take the garbage out of the building. I go to the boiler and check the boiler."

He points to his small apartment. "Here I got leak in the stove, the mirror is no good, my television is damaged, the light no work . . . it is DC.* My radio is bad. I got no telephone. The light is no good. The sink leaks. The window no good. No glass in the window. Nobody comes to make nothing about the insects . . . to this day, nobody . . . many *cucaracha,** nobody to come clean up this

---

DC—direct current. Most appliances and lights operate on AC, alternating current.

cucaracha—Spanish for cockroach.

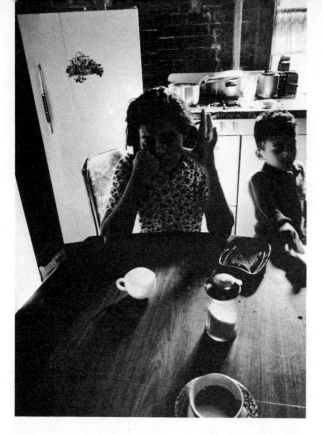

After renovation, a new stove and refrigerator make only a slight change in the lives of the tenants. (Julio Mitchel)

place. I put plaster behind the sink because of a rat hole. There's a rat in there. At night, all the night the people no sleep. Too many noise all the night, too many. The street is full of people all the night. This place is too hot in the summer. It is ninety degrees. The people don't sleep. Sometimes this street is cleaned, but when I came here it was too bad. Garbage in all places."

The neighborhood remains the same, littered with trash neglected. (Julio Mitchel)

Ask him how often he gets out of the house and if his wife has any complaints and Rodriguez will tell you:

"My wife is good woman, domestic woman. She make all work in my house. She can no go out. She get up at six o'clock in the morning. She work to ten or eleven o'clock at night cooking, washing, cleaning."

Petra Rodriguez is a strong-looking, forty-five-year-old woman whose chiseled features give her an almost classical appearance. She is thin and her slender hands move gently even though they are scraped and worn from the hard household chores she performs. Like her husband's, her face is sad, almost fixed in an expression of enduring pain. She rarely smiles. She ties together her thick long black hair in a pony tail with a single rubber band. She wears no lipstick or powder and her face is pale from lack of sunlight. She speaks from inside her kitchen:

"My father was a farmer and I worked on the farm," she begins in answer to a question about her background. She grew up near Rio Piedras, the town in Puerto Rico from which her husband came. "We all worked, my seventeen brothers and sisters. We grew sweet potatoes, bananas, yams, tomatoes. I worked on the farm until I was twenty-five years old. I was raised in the country and I never went to school. I never learned to read or write. I met my husband when I was twenty-five."

Why did she come to New York?

"We had a bad house in Puerto Rico," she says. "My husband, Marcello, used to drink a lot. We fought all the time. So I came over with some of the children. Later he came with the others. When we first came we lived downtown. Our super* had a brother who lived in this building. He told us about the job of super in this building so we came here. Marcello left the factory in New Jersey to become a super here. He didn't like it because this building is bad to be super."

Why don't she and her family move out?

"I live here," she replies, shrugging her shoulders, "because I can't move out. If I were able to move, I would have already. I always liked it down-town, near Delancey Street. I don't like it here be-cause, for people like me with a lot of children, there are so many people with bad habits and there are a lot of drugs. Once in a while I go out. I have a lot of relatives here but I don't visit them. I have only once visit a brother who lives on 104th Street. I also leave the house when they send for me from school. From here I don't go any place. In this building I have lived for two years and I don't know anybody."

FURTHER INQUIRY

1. Is it fair to regard the Rodriguez family's problems as typical of those of slum dwell-ers? Why or why not?
2. Why does Mrs. Rodriguez say she can't move, even though she wants to?
3. Why does the family seem to find life hard-er here than in Puerto Rico?
4. How do the people who first moved in differ from those living at 311 today? How do you account for the change?

---

super—a shortened form of superintendent.

In this selection from the author's well-known book on poverty, he writes about the slums of the past and the "new" slums that are being created daily. If it is true that no one sets out to build a slum, how are slums created?

4

Old Slums, New Slums

by MICHAEL HARRINGTON

WHEN you leave the subway at the Marcy Street stop in Williamsburg, the first thing you notice is a Spanish record playing, Spanish titles on the movie marquee, Spanish shops along the street. But then, next to these signs of the Puerto Rican migrants, there are the shops with Hebrew lettering on the window. And down the street there is the center for remnants of an old German community. There is "integration" here—some of the tenements house Negroes, Puerto Ricans, and whites—but it is the integration of poverty, of rootless transients,* of disintegration.

---

transients—people who are just passing through.

From *The Other America* by Michael Harrington (New York: Macmillan, 1963), pp. 143–45. Copyright © 1963 by Michael Harrington. Reprinted with permission of The Macmillan Company.

Tenements of the Lower East Side in New York City in the early 1900's. (Photograph by Jacob A. Riis; the Jacob A. Riis Collection, Museum of the City of New York)

As a young priest at Holy Trinity sees his parish, it is made up of people on relief and of workers with low-paying jobs, many of them in the garment industry. There are three or four children to a family (the most typical family in the American culture of poverty has seven or more members), but those who stayed behind in the German community have not produced much of a neighborhood social life. There are few clubs, and the church is the center of what community life there is. The people, the priest continues, are very worried because a . . . project is moving into the neighborhood and will uproot them.

Down the street, at a community center, a social worker has a different perspective. For him the large fact is that 6,000 people have moved out in

the recent past. The poor among them have gone to other slums, the better off to the suburbs. (In every slum in New York there is a group of people who have fairly decent incomes but who stay behind out of attachment to a neighborhood, a school, a church.) Since 1955, there has been a steady influx of Negroes and Puerto Ricans, and all this movement has produced an environment of social disintegration and with it violent gangs like the Phantom Lords and the Hell Burners. There is a low-cost housing project nearby, but the natural leaders have been evicted because their income rose too quickly for the legal maximum.

Perhaps the most spectacular and visible effect of this transition is juvenile delinquency. In his study of the New York gangs, Harrison Salisbury

quoted a police estimate that there are 8,000 young people actively engaged in violent anti-social conduct, and another 100,000 who live on the verge of this underworld, shuttling between it and the rest of society. Significantly, the gangs Salisbury described were often integrated, for this integration is regularly a basic component of these neighborhoods of transience.

Thus, the new form of the old slum. If the ethnic slum had been a narrow world of a single religion,

In the old tenements on the Lower East Side in New York, the names on storefronts reveal a mixture of many nationalities. (Wide World)

language, and culture, it was also a goal towards the outside world. This new type of slum groups together failures, rootless people, those born in the wrong time, those at the wrong industry, and the minorities. It is "integrated" in many cases, but in a way that mocks the idea of equality: the poorest and most miserable are isolated together without consideration of race, creed, or color. They are practically forbidden any real relationship with the rest of society.

FURTHER INQUIRY

1. According to the author, how do new slums differ from old slums?
2. Why are the problems of the new slums more difficult to solve?
3. What characteristics other than poverty do the poor of the new slums have in common?
4. Why do people worry about a project being built in their neighborhood?

This selection is taken from the author's book "Prelude to Riot." Here he describes the housing in the black ghetto of Watts in Los Angeles, where one of the nation's largest riots occurred in August, 1965. Why is poor housing often a prelude to riot?

5

Watts—The "Right" Part of Town

by PAUL JACOBS

THE university professor was in his office when the phone rang. The department secretary told him the police wanted to talk to him. When he answered the phone, a police sergeant said that three teen-age Negro boys had been picked up, just outside the university grounds, driving a very old car and claiming to be on their way to the university for an appointment with the professor. "The officer who spotted the kids thought there was something suspicious about them, so he stopped them. When they ran a make on them, they found out that one

From *Prelude to Riot* by Paul Jacobs (New York: Vintage, 1968), pp. 130–32, 145–47. Copyright © 1968 by Random House, Inc. Reprinted with permission of Random House, Inc.

of the three had a record. But they say they were
coming out to see you. Is that right?"

"Yes," answered the professor wearily. "They're
helping me with a project and usually I meet them
not far from where they live. They're all right."

"Well, I'm sorry if we've caused any trouble,"
apologized the officer. "It's just that those kids were
in the wrong part of town, and so naturally our men
are suspicious."

The "right" part of town for Negroes in Los
Angeles, in which it isn't considered "naturally"
suspicious for them to be, is the area lying in the
southern and southeastern parts of the city. The
outside borders of that area are expanding continuously, spreading out like an inkblot, growing
larger and larger each year, frightening more and
more whites into hasty flight to the suburbs. But
despite the outward expansion of the quarter, more
and more Negroes are living inside it, making the
area into a potentially explosive magazine of frustration, bitterness, and anger.

Segregated living is central to the existence of
Negroes in all America, whether they are very poor
or upper-middle-class; no matter how far away they
work—as a drugstore clerk in the central part of the
city, as a porter at the county general hospital in
the northeast section, a welder at the automobile
plant in the southeast, an assembler at the new toy
factory in the southwest area, or as a maid in the
rich section directly west, where a curious little boy
waits with his mother at a bus stop—they live together. Whether or not they want to, the overwhelming majority of Negroes in the cities live within the
confines of the Negro ghetto. They shop in the ghetto and their children go to schools there. Only the

very rich, those who can afford $65,000 houses, can escape the ghetto.

The poorest Negroes in Los Angeles live in public housing projects in the Central, Watts, and Avalon districts, all in the east and southeast; the richest live in private homes in Baldwin Hills, up in the hills at the western boundary of the areas. There, every Christmas, the middle- and upper-class residents decorate the exteriors of their homes, keeping up the tradition begun years ago by middle-class whites. The brilliant beads of lights outlining the houses can be seen from all over Los Angeles, and people come from miles away to drive slowly through the curved and hilly streets, oh-ing and ah-ing at the expensive ways in which the houses have been converted into Christmas decorations. But the people who live there know the neighborhood is slowly becoming all-Negro.

The lives of the Negroes in the big houses up in the hills have very little in common with the lives of those jammed together in the flatlands. Over on Central Avenue the markets sell chitterlings, chicken necks, and grits, and the teen-age boys sit for hours in the "process" shop, getting their hair processed; in the Baldwin Hills district the shopping centers are hardly distinguishable from those in the San Fernando Valley, where hundreds of thousands of white middle-class people live. The recreation and social life of the poor Negroes who live in Watts and Avalon center around the storefront church, the drive-in or hamburger joint, and the pool hall, while up in the hills the richer Negro girls and their boy friends in three-button suits drive off to tea dances in the old mansions on Adams Boulevard, now converted into Negro versions of white country clubs.

Yet suddenly in August 1965 all the Negroes in Los Angeles, the few rich, the larger middle and working classes, and the very many poor, everybody who lived in the ghetto, were linked together: the police and the National Guard drew up boundaries for them, describing what was inside the lines as the

The "right" part of town for Mexican Americans in Los Angeles is the east section, where they live in dilapidated shacks. (Wide World)

"curfew area." For five days it mattered very little whether a man who lived inside that curfew area was the owner of a store or its unemployed looter, whether a woman was a social worker or a social welfare recipient, whether a high school kid was an honor student or a dropout—all were Negroes, and

79

color was the single test of what they could do and where they could go. And the same thing has happened after upheavals in Newark, Detroit, and other cities.

.   .   .

Even in Watts, one of the poorer Negro areas, you can drive down streets and see men mowing the lawns in front of their houses or women stopping to gossip before getting into their cars. It's hard to conceive of such a street as being part of a slum, for it looks as if it were any lower-middle-class street in America. But the very next street will look quite different: seedy, run-down, more like the one described by a Negro woman who owns three houses in Watts: "Watts is a pretty bad old neighborhood. It's not a neighborhood where people would love to be too well, because we have too many broken-down bad houses and unkept homes and things of that kind. We do need a better system in Watts than what we have. What I would say would be better than anything else, we need people to go through Watts and take inventory of what is there and how these places are set up and what the people are doing. The people don't have decent homes to stay in and a lot of people don't know that. The people who would be able to do something

---

Living in a ghetto does not necessarily mean living in a slum in an overcrowded tenement house. Side by side are well-kept houses and broken-down, uncared-for dwellings *(left)*.   (Douglas House Foundation)

about Watts, they don't come there, they don't know about these things. Now, all around where I am living now the yards and the lawns, which is the same thing, is all very unkept."

And what cannot be seen from a car window is how crowded some of the houses are inside, or how some of the garages and sheds fronting on the back alleys are being used to house people under the most primitive conditions, without heat, running water, or toilets. This jamming of human beings into spaces designed originally for horses and cars began during the wartime housing shortage, when whites as well as Negroes and Mexican-Americans suffered from having to pay high rates for garage accommodations. But when the war ended and the postwar housing shortage eased, the whites were able to move into the thousands of apartments and tract homes that shot up almost overnight all over the city and its suburbs.

Ten times as many people live in the Negro sections of Los Angeles as in the white areas. In the ghetto the lowest density of population in 1960 was 10,419 persons per square mile and the highest 14,348 persons. But in Los Angeles County as a whole, which means the figures for the Negro area are included, the average density was only 1,479 persons per square mile!

"Living at home is lousy," says one young man now going to junior college, "not because my mother treats me badly. She doesn't. But it's so damned crowded, I don't have room to turn around. Like, I'm sleeping in one room with my three brothers, and my two sisters are sleeping in the next room with my mother. I'm on a cot, so I'm lucky. Two of my brothers sleep on a sofa and the other one on a mattress.

"How am I supposed to study or write some paper? I was a hell of a lot better off when I was living in a room by myself. But I haven't got enough bread to make it by myself and still go to college. If I want to live alone, I got to go out and hustle. Then I could help out with my mother, too. But if I want to go to school some more, I got to stay at home, and it's lousy. . . ."

FURTHER INQUIRY

1. Why were the police suspicious of the boys? Was such precaution justified? Why or why not?
2. Why is the "right" part of town for blacks really the "wrong" part of town?
3. "The lives of the Negroes in the big houses up in the hills have very little in common with the lives of those jammed together in the flatlands." Why is this?
4. In Watts people are now living in spaces once provided for horses. How do you account for this?
5. Why are tensions likely to be high in Watts and in other black ghettos?

In this selection, the author describes the living conditions in a slum to which she gives the name Eastville, where many Puerto Ricans live when they first move to New York City. Compare the conditions described here with those described by Jacob Riis on pages 51-54.

6

Up from Puerto Rico

by ELENA PADILLA

APARTMENTS, as a rule, are self-contained, having two to seven rooms, including a closet toilet. A bathtub may be located in the kitchen–dining room, which may also be a passage to the rest of the apartment. The enamel lid covering the tub is frequently the utility table. Some rooms have no windows or any other source of ventilation, and are almost as dark in the daytime as at night. The rooms of these apartments are generally so small that they seem overcrowded with only a few pieces of furniture in them. The 1950 census* reported that there was an average of three persons to a

---

census—a count of the population taken every ten years by the government.

From *Up from Puerto Rico* by Elena Padilla (New York: Columbia University Press, 1958), pp. 7–8. Reprinted with permission.

Residents of East Harlem decorate a wall to add a little color to their neighborhood. (Joe Molnar)

The battle against the rats! This photo is used in a television commercial dramatizing the horrifying problem. (Irwin Horowitz, New York City Department of Health)

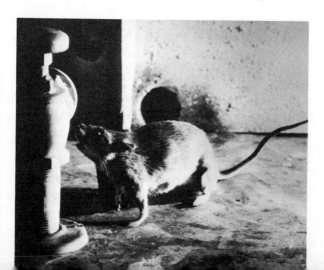

room in the neighborhood. While two or three persons may use a single room, including the kitchen and the living room, as sleeping quarters, there is actually less crowding in Eastville than in comparable slums in other parts of New York, where a whole family may have only one room as its total housing. The latter is rare in Eastville. There, the household consists of an apartment of more than one room. . . .

Often it is up to Eastville tenants themselves to plaster holes in the walls to keep the rats from entering their homes. Alicia Colar, a twelve-year-old

What does a slum family do when the toilet won't flush? when the floor caves in? (Joe Molnar)

girl, was making her bed before going to school one morning. As she shook out the sheets, a rat fell from her bed. She was frightened and ran from the room screaming. Her father simply brought plaster and covered a crack in the wall through which the animal had come into the apartment. Rat extermination campaigns, however, frequently serve only to exacerbate* Eastville's discontent, for the rodents, trying to quench the thirst produced by the poison they have consumed, go out into the streets,

---

exacerbate—worsen.

Bad housing robs children of places to play and exposes them to dangers and accidents in glass- and rock-filled backyards. (Joe Molnar)

the corridors, and the sidewalks, and there they die. This litter remains to rot and decay. Repairing electric installations and defective plumbing, painting, and decorating apartments frequently must be undertaken at the tenant's own expense. Landlords and real estate agencies managing the housing are absentee, and the superintendents, who are the intermediaries with the landlords, often displace the responsibility on to them for the dilapidated conditions. After successive complaints have failed, tenants may either make the repairs themselves, complain to the city authorities, or just live with conditions as they are. In winter, apartments equipped with central heating may be as cold as those that do not have it. Hot water may be turned off for several hours during the day and the evening. In summer, the sticky weather and the warmth exuded by hot water pipes in the walls of apartments and halls combine with the smell of garbage and defective plumbing to push Eastvillers, like other slum dwellers past and present, out of their homes into the streets, where the atmosphere is apt to be cooler and more fragrant.

FURTHER INQUIRY

1. Who is responsible for conditions in Eastville, the landlords or the tenants? Why?
2. How is Eastville better or worse than other slums?
3. Why does the attempt to kill rats often make conditions worse?
4. Is there an "Eastville" in the town or city in which you live? Is one developing? Describe the circumstances that may make it develop.

This well-known author comments on the attitude of Harlem Negroes toward the housing projects that have been built in an effort to eliminate slums. "A ghetto can be improved in one way only: out of existence," Baldwin says. What does he mean?

7

Harlem Projects

by JAMES BALDWIN

THE projects in Harlem are hated. They are hated almost as much as policemen, and this is saying a great deal. They are hated for the same reason: both reveal, unbearably, the real attitude of the white world, no matter how many liberal speeches are made, no matter how many civil rights commissions are set up.

The projects are hideous, of course, there being a law, apparently respected throughout the world, that popular housing shall be as cheerless as a prison. They are lumped all over Harlem, colorless, bleak, high, and revolting. The wide windows look out on Harlem's invincible and indescribable squalor:

From *Nobody Knows My Name* by James Baldwin (New York: Dial Press, 1965), pp. 63–65. Copyright 1954, © 1956, 1958, 1959, 1960, 1961 by James Baldwin and used by permission of the publisher, The Dial Press, Inc.

Riverton, a Harlem project—clean, neat, and dehumanizing. (Shalmon Bernstein)

the Park Avenue railroad tracks, around which, about forty years ago, the present dark community began; the unrehabilitated houses, bowed down, it would seem, under the great weight of frustration and bitterness they contain; the dark, the ominous schoolhouses from which the child may emerge maimed, blinded, hooked, or enraged for life; and the churches, churches, block upon block of churches, niched in the walls like cannon in the walls of a fortress. Even if the administration of the projects were not so insanely humiliating (for example: One must report raises in salary to the management, which will then eat up the profit by raising one's rent; the management has the right to know who is staying in your apartment; the management can ask you to leave, at their discretion), the

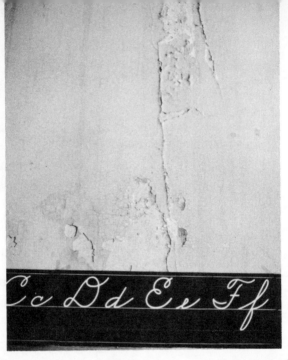

Many slum schools, like the homes, are badly in need of repair. (Joe Molnar)

projects would still be hated because they are an insult to the meanest intelligence.

Harlem got its first private project, Riverton—which is now, naturally, a slum—about twelve years ago because at that time Negroes were not allowed to live in Stuyvesant Town.* Harlem watched Riverton go up, therefore, in the most violent bitterness of spirit, and hated it long before the builders arrived. They began hating it at about the time people began moving out of their condemned houses to make

Stuyvesant Town—a housing development in mid-Manhattan.

room for this additional proof of how thoroughly the white world despised them. And, they had scarcely moved in, naturally, before they began smashing windows, [and] defacing walls. . . . Liberals, both black and white, were appalled at the spectacle. I was appalled by the liberal innocence—or cynicism which comes out in practice as much the same thing. Other people were delighted to be able to point to proof positive that nothing could be done

A Harlem church—"nicked in the walls like a cannon in the walls of a fortress."

Lenox Terrace. A modern, clean, and comfortable apartment building, occupied by middle-class Negroes in New York's Harlem, more nearly resembles the dwellings of middle-class whites than those of the majority of Harlem Negroes, who live in rat-infested slums. (Joe Molnar)

to better the lot of the colored people. They were, and are, right in one respect: that nothing can be done as long as they are treated like colored people. The people in Harlem know they are living there because white people do not think they are good enough to live anywhere else. No amount of "improvement" can sweeten this fact. Whatever money is now being earmarked to improve this, or any other ghetto, might as well be burnt. A ghetto can be improved in one way only: out of existence.

FURTHER INQUIRY

1. Why does Baldwin say that housing projects are hated? Do you know people who live in projects? Do they hate them? What reasons do they give?
2. What alternatives to housing projects can you suggest? Justify your suggestions.
3. Why must salary increases be reported to the management of housing projects? Is this fair? Why or why not?

"To live in public housing in Los Angeles has become a mark of shame . . . ," says the author of this selection. Here he describes all the rules and regulations under which tenants in housing projects live and the tensions that invasion of privacy creates. How can public housing become a source of pride rather than shame?

8

Los Angeles Projects

by PAUL JACOBS

"**W**HEN you move in a project, you must have twenty-five-dollar deposit," explains a tenant. "He must have the amount of rent from you. Well, if it's the first of the month, so then he has a certain amount, and if it's in the middle of the month, well, then he have the rest of the month plus twenty-five dollars. So this is a strain on you because you must have eight dollars more for garbage cans and water hose. So it's eight dollars, twenty-five dollars, and then the rent and lights if you have to have them transferred, or you might

From *Prelude to Riot* by Paul Jacobs (New York: Vintage, 1968), pp. 160–65, 168–69. Copyright © 1968 by Random House, Inc. Reprinted with permission of Random House, Inc.

never had lights, then you got to do that, too, this in the beginning is a strain, you know. You gotta have all of this stuff before you get in. And they don't take part of it. You have to have it all. Then after you move in, they give you the rules and regulations."

The "rules and regulations" which the Housing Authority attempts to use to control the tenants encompass nearly every detail of daily life. Tenants who do not put trash cans out alongside the house are charged for having it done by the maintenance crews; tenants who don't clean up their own yards are charged for having that done. If a maintenance man decides a lawn needs watering and turns on the hose, the tenant is charged for that; if a stove is broken and it is the property of the Authority, the tenant is charged for the repairs. The tenants may put only those screen doors on the apartments which are supplied and installed by the Authority, and they must pay for both the door and installation at the usual commercial rates. "We must have uniformity in the project so that the apartments all look more or less alike," says the director. His words are echoed by a member of his top staff, explaining why the tenants are not permitted to put up their own screen doors: "We want to keep a standard position instead of having someone put up an oddball type of screen. If all the doors didn't look alike, it would be an unsightly appearance."

"The kids can't climb the trees and they can't even play on the grass in front of the house," bitterly complains a mother. "If the kids get out there and play ball and put a spot out there, the housing, they charge you to put the grass out there. So then if you tell the kids to play ball in front where you can watch them, it's your own risk if someone breaks a window, say, if they bat a ball and break my window, that's seven dollars and sixty cents. So I get worried when I see the kids playing out front, and I holler at them and they holler back and run over to the parking lot to play. That's where they can learn to strip cars—that parking lot. That's an awful position for kids to be in."

The principal of an elementary school a few blocks from a housing project in East Los Angeles explains how one of the teachers brings her cat to school so that little children can see and touch the cat. Wide-eyed, the little boys and girls tentatively stroke the cat as it stirs in the teacher's arms. *"El gato,* look at *el gato,"* they say wonderingly, as other children might speak of a giraffe or tiger at the zoo.

"In the project, no one is allowed to have a pet," explains the principal, "and so these kids come to school without ever having had much contact with pets. Dogs and cats are strange to them."

.   .   .

"Once, years ago, the manager of one project set aside a piece of land near a dump yard on the project," says an old-timer on the administration staff, "and the families had a vegetable garden, a flower garden, and the kids had animals up there. The kids would take turns to go up there and take care of them, they would feed them and this was a good experience for them, but, of course, that got knocked out. A new man came in and he said it was too much trouble and they needed the yard for something else, for maintenance or something."

Still, not all the projects are places in which the description of "suicide" is apt. A few of them never have any vacancies: the smaller ones, with fewer people in them; more centrally located, they are

Public housing is a mixed blessing. Negro children at play in front of the Hunter's Point housing project in San Francisco. Not a tree or a flower is visible.   (UPI)

spread out over larger areas, and they have better facilities for children and more sympathetic managers. A few of the larger projects, where the managers attempt to establish some channels of communication with the tenants, are better than the prison camps which most of the projects resemble.

Of all the Housing Authority's rules and regulations, two disturb the tenants more than all the rest. Under the regulations the tenants have very little privacy: members of the project staff have the right to enter the tenants' apartments to make inspections for repairs and check on the general conditions of refrigerators or items of furniture which the tenants may be renting from the Authority. In some projects the tenants are not advised in advance of the forthcoming visit, and in others the tenants are convinced that the staff members interfere far more than they should in their personal lives.

"When we first moved into an apartment here, I had put in a request for something to be fixed," one tenant reports typically, "and I was in my bed sleeping a few days after. It was early in the morning when the man first came in. And I was in the bed. And I got so mad, I couldn't say anything, you know. I told him, excuse me, 'Get the hell out of here until I get up and get me some clothes on.' And he said, 'Well, I'm sorry, lady, but you put in a request and I'm here to do my job.' And I said, 'But that don't give you the right to open my door and come in here to my house when I'm in bed.' But he wasn't sorry, he just kept saying, 'Well, lady, I have a job to do.' And I told him, 'Well, I pay rent. I pay rent here in this apartment and it don't give you the right to use your key and come in. You give me the chance to get up and open the door.' "

Another describes her experience: "A man from the office come and told me to take my ham bone out of the icebox. I had paid nine dollars for a ham and we had trimmed it all down to the bone, and I was saving the bone to cook with some beans. He wanted me to take it out. He came to the house for something, to inspect. They got a key. They walk in when they get good and ready! They don't have to inform you; they come. He walk in when he good and ready and he looks in the icebox—well, the icebox belongs to the house, but the bone don't belong to the house. So he told me that the bone shouldn't been in there because it was dried and this kind of stuff. And I said, 'Who in the hell are you talking to? I paid nine dollars for that ham, and if I want to keep it until next Easter, then I'm going to keep the bone.' So we went round and round about that."

The director of the Authority justifies the need to enter the tenants' apartments in these terms: "We don't like regimentation but at the same time we can't let them live in filth. And as to maintenance, the men are invited in when the tenants make a report, like, they've got a stoppage. If the maintenance man goes up, knocks on the door, and no one is home, he knocks on the door three times distinctly. Then we unlock the door with a master key, stick our head in and holler 'Maintenance man,' and then proceed with the work that's to be done. Now snooping, no. But we do have to look into our own refrigerators because I've seen them iced up where you could hardly get the door shut, and we have to see that kept up."

. . .

The sliding scale of rents, based on income and the number of people in the family, is also a source of continual tension between the tenants and the

Authority. When the projects were the temporary homes for tenants whose incomes were on the rise, the sliding scale was of no great significance. But as the ceiling on income forced these groups out of the projects and they were replaced by tenants whose incomes were fixed at very low levels, either because they were low-paid unskilled workers or because their income was in the low levels of the public assistance program, the sliding scale began to be seen as a penalty when some slight increase in income occurred or when the size of the family increased.

"Now, if you're on a job, next month you might get a raise. Now when you get a three-cent raise on your job, you get a six-dollar raise on house rent. So then, we're in this place but we have certain things we can't do in our own home while we're paying rent. For instance, you can't come and visit me no more than two weeks. If you stay longer than that, they'll assume that you live there and you have to start paying some rent."

The tenants in the projects reiterate again and again their bitter complaints about the rents, for they see the increase as a penalty for attempting to raise the standard of their living, a handicap to bringing themselves out of the low-income levels to higher ones. If, for example, the teen-age son gets a job delivering newspapers, the amount he earns is added to the family income and the rent increases. And even though the rent increase is only 20 to 25 per cent of the increase in income, it is resented: it represents to the tenants the government's taking away from them something they have earned.

Without doubt, however, the group most strongly resentful of the Housing Authority's rental policies are the great number of people whose sole or major

source of income is from the public assistance programs. Their lives are under the double controls of
the Authority and the welfare department. They
see that the Housing Authority sets a flat rent for
them which may be higher than that charged for
identical apartments whose tenants are not on public
assistance. For example, a family consisting of a
mother and three children, with the mother working or getting unemployment insurance, may pay
less for rent than a family of the same size whose
income is derived from the Aid to Dependent Children Program. In addition, any time welfare increases the family's monthly allowance the rent is
increased, too. In some situations it is even possible
for a family on public assistance to be charged more
rent by the Authority than is allotted it by the welfare department, with the result that money must be
taken from the already meager food budget to pay
the rent.

"Let me tell what happened," says one of the tenants in a project. "The City Housing Authority and
the welfare department sign an agreement that the
county would allow so much for rent, and Housing
would get it. Now, when I first moved into the project, my rent was forty-one dollars a month. I was
working. Then I got a three-cent raise, and my rent
went to forty-six dollars a month. Then when I got
sick and couldn't work no more, I was placed on
the county, and my rent went to fifty-eight dollars
per month. Then I got a two-dollar raise on the
county check and it went to sixty dollars a month.
In most cases, you pay more money for rent if
you're on the county. It came about because of an
agreement two people signed.

"But this is the point I don't understand. Say, for
instance, they come and give you a two-dollar raise

on your check, like the cost of living is high. What good is it going to do you? You're still in bad shape. You still can't get the things you want to eat 'cause they, the Housing Authority, got it."

. . .

And so the endless downward-spiralling process continues in the projects. To live in public housing in Los Angeles has become a mark of shame, for it means that one has no effective voice in determining the conditions of his own life in one of its most important aspects—the living space that each human being needs. Inside the projects there are some community activities going on that involve some of the tenants; and the overwhelming majority of the tenants are decent people, trying hard to make decent homes for themselves and their children. But they must live in close contact with the antisocial personalities who flourish in such atmospheres. And because the projects are so often isolated, even within the ghettos, they become havens and sanctuaries for the hoodlums and criminals of the area who use the projects as their own base of operations, the parking lots as a place to strip cars, the playground for glue sniffing, the bushes as a cover from which to venture out to snatch a purse and flee to a waiting car.

And unless the mother or the parents are able to battle continuously against almost overwhelming enemies for the minds and souls of their families, the children of the projects grow up in a world in which government is the enemy and society is only a large replica of the jungle the projects have become.

Segregated housing in the cities is the most visible manifestation of the social disease from which America suffers; segregated public housing in the cities shows the disease in its most virulent and noxious form. And the existence of segregated public housing is the fault of the government, just as government must accept a major portion of the blame for the continuation of segregation in private housing.

FURTHER INQUIRY

1. How would you like to live under the rules and regulations that are described here?
2. To what extent, if any, do you agree that the Housing Authority is justified in entering apartments unannounced?
3. "Now when you get a three-cent raise on your job, you get a six-dollar raise on house rent," says one tenant. While he may be exaggerating, what complaint is he echoing? Is such a complaint justified? Why or why not?
4. Should pets be allowed in housing developments? Justify your point of view.
5. If "projects" are not the answer for housing for the poor, what alternatives may be suggested?

In this book, the U. S. Senator from New York writes about discrimination in the United States. Having himself come from an immigrant background, he feels deeply about the problem. Here he writes about discrimination in housing. Does one who has experienced discrimination understand it better? Is he likely to be more or less tolerant of others?

9

Discrimination, U.S.A.

by JACOB K. JAVITS

A WHOLE sad mythology has developed around the subject of minority occupancy and property values. The contention that values will depreciate* with the entry of a minority into a neighborhood is so widespread and well established that it amounts to an article of faith. Yet there is a wealth of scientific evidence to refute that conclusion.

During the course of the three-year study by the Commission on Race and Housing, an investigation of the effects of nonwhite entry on property values was conducted in seven cities on both coasts and in mid-continent. The Commission found that the entry

---

depreciate—drop in value.

From *Discrimination, U.S.A.* by Jacob K. Javits (New York: Washington Square Press, 1962), pp. 131–33.

"Suppose a Negro family moved next door to you. What would you do?" The surprising response of whites:

	East	Mid-west	South	West	Adults	Youth
			Percentages			
Accept them, welcome them, treat them like white people, be a good neighbor	22	19	13	21	19	33
Would stay here	13	14	12	9	12	6
Would do nothing at all	35	30	25	40	31	29
Depends (on the kind of people they are, etc.)	12	8	8	10	9	10
Would dislike it, wouldn't socialize, but generally do nothing about it	6	11	10	8	9	10
Would move, sell, get out, etc.	9	15	23	12	15	11
Miscellaneous	1	1	4	*	2	2
Don't know, no answer	3	3	7	2	4	4

* Less than 1 percent.
Totals may exceed 100 percent because of a few multiple answers.

of nonwhites had either a favorable effect or no effect at all on property values in the majority of cases.

If white residents panic, and a mass exodus ensues, the expectation of a fall in property values becomes a "self-fulfilling prophecy," the Commission reported. In this case, it is the mass exodus rather than the entrance of a minority that gluts the market and depresses values. It is comparable to a bank run engendered by fears. On the other hand, if the white residents do not yield to the "myths" but behave in normal fashion, the pressure for nonwhite housing may bid prices up. It has been clearly demonstrated that in the many integrated neighborhoods where the concern is for good neighbors, regardless of race or creed, values remain stable.

There is an old cliché that nothing is sure but death and taxes. The wise man would head the list of certainties with the word "change." The face of American neighborhoods has been changing from the day the pilgrims landed. Harry Golden, author of *Only in America* and *For 2¢ Plain,* gives one of the best modern and classic descriptions of the inexorable change in neighborhood composition in a "nation on the move." He tells of a visit to the cold-water tenement which was his childhood home on the Lower East Side of New York City. It had been forty years since his last visit to the neighborhood, but [he] found the building still standing and still full of tenants. Golden writes:

I examined the names on the mailboxes, and where once they had been Rabinowitz and Cohen, they were now Perez and Amici. And as I stood in that hallway where I had spent my first fifteen years, the Negro and Puerto Rican kids looked at me as if I had just dropped down from the planet Mars.

You can write a social history of our country by just walking through these neighborhoods. First there were the Germans, then the Irish, followed by the Jews, then the Italians, and now the Negroes and Puerto Ricans. . . . What manner of children, of what nationality and history, will be staring at the "stranger" when the Puerto Rican novelist or Negro Vice President of the United States comes back fifty years from now? . . . I am certain that "This scene [will] be acted over . . . and in accents yet unborn."

The term "changing neighborhood"—meaning a neighborhood in racial transition—has come to be synonymous with "problem neighborhood" in the minds of too many people. Whether or not it is indeed a problem area is squarely up to its residents and to the city officials charged with the proper administration of the building codes. In the normal course of events, new neighbors of like income and cultural background will move into a given area. Granted, of course, that landlords are not permitted to put ten families into living quarters which were designed for one!

Change, as such, is nothing to be feared. What must be countered is panic and flight and the likely result in overcrowding of the newcomers and property deterioration. The state of Maryland, in such a case, suspended the licenses of two Baltimore real estate operators for three months after the Real Estate Commission found that they had "engaged in a continued and flagrant course of misrepresentation" and in "misleading and untruthful advertising." It was charged that these men had deliberately engaged in activities calculated to incite panic selling in a racially changing neighborhood.

FURTHER INQUIRY

1. According to the Senator, what effect does the entry of nonwhites into formerly all-white neighborhoods have on property values?
2. What is meant by a "self-fulfilling prophecy"?
3. Why does the author quote Harry Golden on the subject of "changing neighborhoods"?
4. Is "neighborhood change" inevitable? Why or why not?

In their book, the authors describe the relationship between housing and laws against discrimination in housing. The authors are sociologists who have written widely on urban minority group problems; Mr. Moynihan is serving the Nixon administration as Presidential Assistant for Urban Affairs. Here the authors describe why racial ghettos develop despite laws designed to prevent them.

10

Housing and the Law

by NATHAN GLAZER *and*
DANIEL PATRICK MOYNIHAN

T HE Negro ghetto in New York City has not dis-
solved, neither in Manhattan nor in the other
boroughs, for the poor or the well-to-do. The ghetto
is not surrounded by a sharp line, and there is less
sense of boundaries in New York than there is in
many other cities. But in each of the four main boroughs there is a single concentrated area of Negro
settlement, shading off at the edge to mixed areas,

From *Beyond the Melting Pot* by Nathan Glazer and Daniel
Patrick Moynihan (Cambridge, Mass.: The M.I.T. Press, 1963),
pp. 54–56. Copyright © 1963 by The Massachusetts Institute of
Technology and the President and Fellows of Harvard College
Reprinted by permission of The M.I.T. Press.

which tend with the increase in Negro population to become as concentratedly Negro as the centers. If one looks at a map of New York City on which the places of residence of the Negro population have been spotted, one will find many areas with small percentages of Negroes, and it may look as if the Negro population is spreading evenly through the city, is being "integrated." But a closer examination will reveal that these small outlying areas of Negro population are generally areas with public housing projects, and the Negro population is there because the housing projects are there. The projects in the outlying boroughs are partly Negro islands in the white sea.

There are laws forbidding discrimination in renting and selling houses, just as there is a law forbidding discrimination in employment. The city and state laws have steadily increased their coverage to the point where all housing but rooms or apartments in one's own home, and units in two-family homes in which one is occupied by the owner, must be available without discrimination on account of race, religion, or national origin. Ninety-five percent of city housing is now covered by the law. But the law forbidding discrimination in housing is much less effective than the law forbidding discrimination in employment. It is weaker, and provides no specific penalties, though if a landlord remains adamant, the city can bring him into court.

But the main reason why the law against discrimination in housing is less effective in changing this situation than the law against discrimination in employment is that apartments are not controlled by big bureaucratic organizations. The big projects can be prevented from discriminating by law. But most apartments are in existing houses owned by small

Chicago residents protest alleged housing discrimination by real estate dealers. (Wide World)

Projects separate the poor into tiny islands removed from the ghetto. (Fujihira, Monkmeyer)

landlords. Long before the complaint can possibly be acted on, the apartment is gone. There is also little danger in a landlord practicing evasive action. It is fair to say that this is a law to which the run-of-the-mill landlords have responded with massive evasion. It takes elaborate measures really to get an apartment the way the law is now written. One needs a respectable-looking white friend to find out first that the apartment is available; a Negro who really wants it and is ready to take it then asks for it and is told it is not available; a second white is then required in order that he may be told that the apartment is still available, so as to get a sure-fire case; then direct confrontation plus rapid action in reporting all the details to the City Commission on

Human Rights is required. At this point, the landlord will often succumb. The Committee on Racial Equality (CORE) [sic] as well as Reform Democratic clubs and other organizations have supplied the whites for this sandwiching technique, the elaborate advance planning and chance for immediate gratification have supplied perhaps a more satisfying activity to CORE than picketing local branches of Woolworth's. (The white pickets were generally in the majority, and were unhappy at the Negroes going past them.)

Perhaps even more significant in reducing the effectiveness of the law than landlord resistance is the perpetual housing shortage in New York City. This "temporary" situation is now as permanent as anything in life ever is. Someone beginning school in New York City during the Second World War may now be married and having children in a housing market which has the same "temporary" shortage that it had at the end of the war. Even in the absence of discrimination, the low-income tenant would find it very hard to find cheap housing when it is being demolished faster than it is being built. The housing shortage means that we deal with a situation of "discrimination for" as well as "discrimination against." Just as good jobs are reserved for friends, relatives, and insiders, so are good apartments. Indeed, the better apartments in New York descend through a chain of relatives and friends, year after year, decade after decade. The most valuable of these commodities are, of course, the rent-controlled apartments. Rent-controlled apartments mean, as a matter of fact, discrimination against everyone who has come into the city since 1943. Even *without* any discrimination on the ground of color, Negroes (and in larger measure Puerto Ricans) would be

Cheap housing is demolished faster than it is built. (Joe Molnar)

getting a poor share of the housing market, and paying more for it, because they are in larger measure latecomers.

FURTHER INQUIRY

1. How do you define a ghetto? Are there ghettos other than Negro ones? Justify your answer.
2. If there are laws prohibiting housing discrimination, how do you account for the existence of Negro ghettos?
3. How do you account for the difference between the way the law treats private houses and the way it treats apartments?
4. Why is the law forbidding discrimination in housing weaker than the one forbidding discrimination in employment?

This excerpt describes what happened in one community when it was learned that Negroes were about to move in. "The whole place will go black!" was the fear of the community. How do you account for this fear? Have you heard similar fears expressed in your neighborhood?

11

But Not Next Door

by DAVID H. *and* HARRY M. ROSEN

I T was Tuesday evening, November 10, when Bob Danning heard the news about Progressive Development. He was just getting into his car to drive to the drugstore for cigarettes when he was hailed by one of his neighbors, a vestryman* of St. Gregory Episcopal Church. Bob waited for him to approach the car and then listened in stunned silence as his neighbor told him that Negroes would be moving into Deerfield, moving right next door to the church, just a few blocks from their home.

---

vestryman—church official.

From *But Not Next Door* by Harry M. and David H. Rosen (New York: Ivan Obolensky, 1962), pp. 17–21. Copyright © 1962 by Harry M. Rosen and David H. Rosen. Reprinted by permission of Astor-Honor, Inc., New York, N.Y.

After giving Bob the news, the vestryman didn't stop to discuss the matter further, but hurried on home. Bob got into his car and drove slowly to the village. At the drugstore he saw a few people whom he knew casually, and he wondered if they too had heard the news. But he didn't wait to find out. He responded perfunctorily* to a few hellos, purchased his cigarettes, and returned to his home, conscious of being shocked by the news but not knowing why.

Helen Danning was shocked too, when Bob told her about his talk with the vestryman. "Good heavens, Bob," she cried, "the whole place will go black!"

"Not the way I hear it," replied Bob. "The builders have some kind of controlled occupancy system so that they can keep the ratio between black and white fairly constant, about ten or twelve black families to about forty white families. It seems they've been doing the same sort of thing out East."

Helen didn't understand this too well and didn't really care. Negroes were moving into Deerfield—that was the important and fearful fact. She wanted to call her neighbor and friend, Betty, but Bob stopped her. "There's no point in spreading the news all over town and starting a panic," he said. "It may not happen. Besides, there's no need for us to get excited—we'll be moving out of here one of these days, maybe even before the project is finished."

Helen asked about Father Parker's reaction. Bob didn't know. "What can he say, anyway? He's a minister. His job is to preach brotherly love. But I bet he isn't happy about having the problem dumped right on his doorstep!"

---

perfunctorily—automatically.

"What do you mean 'on his doorstep'?" Helen asked.

"I mean just that—on his doorstep," replied Bob. "The sub-divisions are on two sides of the church property."

"You mean they're building those houses on Wilmot?"

"That's right. And there will be more going up north of there on the other side of the church."

"But those houses on Wilmot look enormous—they must cost a fortune!"

"From what I understand, they will sell for $30,000 and up. But what difference does that make?"

Helen seemed relieved, and yet surprised. "There can't be many colored people who can afford to pay that kind of money for a house."

"You'd be surprised," countered Bob. "There are many Negro doctors and lawyers and business-men who can pay $30,000 and more. And they only need ten or so for this development."

"Can the builder really do that?" asked Helen. "After all, isn't that a kind of discrimination?"

By this time, Bob's shock had changed to frustrated anger. "Who cares whether it's discrimination or not?" he cried. "All I know is that there's going to be a big mess in this town, and God knows how long it will last and how it will affect property values! It's less than three blocks away! Can you imagine trying to sell our house for a decent price and explaining to buyers that they have black neighbors only three blocks away?"

Now Helen experienced a different kind of shock. "I don't understand you, Bob. I didn't know you had such strong feelings about colored people. Why,

A homeowner's determined answer to real estate dealers who engage in a campaign to profit from panic selling. (Wide World)

The message of the bomb: Get out!   (Wide World)

just now you sounded like somebody from Little Rock!"*

"It has nothing to do with the way I feel about colored people," answered Bob, and his voice was heavy with despair. "We are going to have to sell this house soon, maybe in just a few months, and we simply can't afford to take any loss. What if we can't sell it at all?"

"Well, who's panicking now?" Helen was trying to be reassuring, as much for herself as for her

---

Little Rock—city in Arkansas where school desegregation problems led to violence.

husband. "Of course, we'll sell it, and why should we have to take a loss? I can't imagine $30,000 homes pulling down values in the neighborhood, regardless of who lives in them!"

"Maybe you're right," said Bob. "Maybe I'm getting excited over nothing." But he didn't sound very convinced.

The Dannings spent a restless night. And when Bob met his usual companions on the train the next morning, he said nothing about Floral Park. Nor did any of his fellow commuters. The word had not yet gotten around.

FURTHER INQUIRY

1. How do you account for the panic created by the news that Negroes were moving into the neighborhood?
2. Why did Bob Danning's wife feel relieved when she heard the price of the houses to be offered?
3. Why did Bob Danning feel that he would have to take a big loss on his own home? Were his fears justified?

In this selection the author describes
what happened to her and her family
when they helped the Wades, a Negro
family, buy a home in a formerly all-
white community. The assistance that the
Bradens gave the Wades was an act of
courage. Why? Would you have had
similar courage?

12

Shots in the Night

by ANNE BRADEN

THE cross burning occurred late Saturday night,
May 15. It was part of a night of terror at the
Wade house that climaxed two days of threats from
residents of the Rone Court area.

At dawn on Friday morning, May 14, the morning after the crowd visited our house, our telephone
rang. I got out of bed to answer, and a woman's
voice, unidentified, spoke:

"Get those niggers out of that house. We won't
have them out here. You put them in there. You
get them out. We'll give you forty-eight hours, or
you take the consequences."

I started to argue with her, but she hung up.

From *The Wall Between* by Anne Braden (New York:
Monthly Review Press, 1958), pp. 63–67. Copyright © 1958 by
Monthly Review Press. Reprinted by permission.

The poor live near their prosperous neighbors, but on the other side of the tracks. (Shalmon Bernstein)

The ringing of the phone had awakened the children, and I went to get Anita out of her bed and change her diaper. I had just time to remove one diaper pin when the phone rang again. This time it was a man's voice.

"We'll give you forty-eight hours. Get those niggers out of that house."

From then on, the phone rang constantly—sometimes the calls were no more than four or five minutes apart. Sometimes there was a tirade from the other end. Sometimes only a brief statement: "You'd better watch out!" "Get the Wades off Rone Court!" I was afraid to let the phone ring, or leave it off the hook, thinking the Wades or someone else with something important to say might call, so I kept on answering—getting the children's breakfast and settling Jimmy in his sandpile and Anita in her playpen outside in between the rings. When Carl got up—he always slept later than the rest of us because of his night-work hours—we took turns answering the calls. Sometimes the caller was a woman; sometimes it was a man. It seemed to me, however, that there were not many different voices. Probably no more than four or five people were doing all the telephoning. And whenever I could catch the phone between rings, I made calls of my own to people I thought might offer the Wades support.

Andrew had no phone at his Rone Court house at that time, but the same kind of calls came to him at his place of business. He remained calm. On Friday he had planned to move the rest of the furniture into the house, and he proceeded with his plans.

First, however, he called the county police, in whose jurisdiction the house lay, and told them of the threats. He talked to the captain of the police district; his father talked to the chief of the county police, Colonel Walter Layman. Both Wades told these men that Andrew was moving into the house on that day, that there had been threats, and asked that police be on hand to nip any trouble in the bud. Both the captain and the police chief replied that they did not have sufficient men on the force to maintain a constant guard, but they said they would patrol the area and be on watch.

If any police car did patrol the area of Rone Court that day, when Andrew was moving his furniture in, or the next afternoon or evening, after he returned to the house, Andrew did not see it.

By Friday night, the furniture was all in the house, but Andrew and his family did not stay there that night. The next morning, our phone rang again early. At 7 o'clock a voice said, "Braden, watch out. Something's going to happen at twelve o'clock." The calls continued at intervals all morning. Close to noon they became more frequent. "Braden, one hour." "Braden, fifty minutes."

About 11 o'clock, Carl was eating his usual combination breakfast and lunch, and I sat down to drink a cup of coffee with him.

"I guess it's all a bluff, don't you suppose?" I asked.

Carl, as usual, was perfectly calm.

"Of course it is," he laughed. "You don't think if they were really going to do something they'd call us up and tell us in advance, do you?" He turned to talk to Jimmy, who was telling him in great detail about the house he had been building in his sandpile. . . .

"Well, maybe we ought to call the police just in case . . . ," I suggested tentatively at the first break of Jimmy's tumble of words.

"Might not be a bad idea," Carl said, paying more attention to the piece of toast and jam he was fixing for Jimmy than he was paying to me. "I'll call them in a little while if you want to."

He finished eating and took his time about washing his breakfast dishes. Finally, he went in the living room and called the city police—our house, unlike Andrew's, was within the city limits—and they said they would send a car to drive by our house around noon. Then Carl sat down in the big chair and relaxed to read the paper. By this time it was 11:45, and the telephone was ringing every few minutes: "Braden, watch out." "Braden, fifteen minutes." Finally I took the phone off the hook.

I looked at Carl, as he sat quietly reading the paper. My mind told me his unconcern was sensible and that the voices on the phone were only trying to scare us. But this business of facing physical threats was something new to me and I had not yet

learned to shrug it off, as I finally did later. And besides, I was not sure—and am still not—just how much of Carl's nonchalance was a reflection of courage and how much of it was pure phlegmatism* in the face of danger. His whole life experience had

---

phlegmatism—calmness.

Integration in northern suburbs often means that not all the whites have moved out yet. (Wide World)

been different from mine. He had grown up in the jungle atmosphere of Louisville's Portland, where the gang of boys on his block was always in a state of running physical warfare with gangs from surrounding blocks. In my world, although I knew now that it was shot through with its own terrible kind of viciousness, it was a viciousness that was

127

always smoothly covered with a façade of gentility and soft voices, where physical violence was something beneath discussion. The violence that permeated the South in those days was far removed from my insulated world—far away and under the cover of darkness, hardly a muted whisper of it reaching the rarefied atmosphere in which I lived. Now that it had burst into my own life, I was startled and dismayed.

The children had followed us into the living room, and I busied myself with them for a few minutes. Anita was sitting on the floor by the long bookcases that lined one wall of the room and gleefully pulled out books—our most precious possession and the one thing in the house that was taboo for the children to touch. I rescued the books and diverted her attention to one of her own picture books. Then I sat down on the arm of Carl's chair.

"Look," I said, "I don't want to be a scary-cat, but don't you think we ought to go out in the yard or something about noon? Suppose they've set a time bomb under the house."

Carl laughed and pulled me down into his lap and kissed me.

"Anne," he said, "you're being silly."

I returned his kiss and got up.

"I know it's silly," I said, "but I don't see any use in being foolish either—not with the children anyway. I'm going to take them out in the yard."

I picked up Anita and suggested to Jimmy that he come out in the back yard and I would push him in his swing. He was delighted, and we left. Carl did not protest, but he shook his head and turned back to his newspaper.

Of course, he was right. I saw the patrol car that the police had promised drive by several times as I pushed Jimmy in the swing. But noon passed, and nothing happened—not at our house.

Late that afternoon, Andrew and Charlotte went to Rone Court to spend their first night in the new house. Because of the threats, they decided to leave their two-year-old daughter, Rosemary, with Andrew's parents for the night, but they took with them a young friend, Carlos Lynes. When they arrived, the front picture window had been broken with a rock: they found the rock inside the living room. Around it was wrapped a piece of paper on which was written "NIGGER GET OUT." Andrew and Carlos Lynes checked around the house. There was no other damage, except that the grating of one of the small air vents under the house was broken out. It was the vent where dynamite was to be placed six weeks later.

The Wades and Lynes spent the evening arranging the furniture in the house. About 10 o'clock they heard a noise outside. Andrew stepped onto a side porch and saw a cross burning in the field next door. Around the cross five figures were dancing. He could see that they were adults, and they looked like men, but he could not make out their faces. One of them shouted: "Get out while you still can!"

Andrew had a gun in his pocket. He pulled it out but then dropped it to his side.

"So—you are burning your own American flag!" he called back to the men. In a few minutes they left.

There was no telephone in the house to call the police or friends. Andrew looked out: there was no police car in sight. Charlotte, who was seven months pregnant, was quite worried. But Andrew told her it would be foolish to leave the house then—in the darkness and alone. The Wades and Lynes settled down for the night, Andrew and Charlotte in the front bedroom and Lynes on a couch they had put temporarily in the kitchen.

At 2 A.M. they were awakened by the sound of rifle shots. About ten shots rang out. There was the noise of glass breaking. Lynes heard one bullet zing past his ear. He dropped to the floor and lay there, waiting until the shooting stopped. Andrew and Charlotte jumped from their bed and ran into the hallway. Andrew pushed Charlotte to the floor and crawled into the kitchen. Looking out the window, he saw a car pulling off about 200 feet away on Crums Lane. The glass in the kitchen door was broken. Bullets were lodged in the woodwork of the pantry. Everything was quiet. There was only the roar of the car's motor as it sped away.

FURTHER INQUIRY

1. What acts of courage may be noted in this selection?
2. Why were the Wades determined to stay in a neighborhood where they were not wanted? Was their decision wise? Why or why not?
3. How do you account for the attitude of the rest of the community?
4. What groups have used the tactics of terror to frighten blacks and other racial or religious minorities?
5. It has been said that violence is as American as cherry pie. Do you agree or disagree? Why? To what extent is this selection representative of the attitude of most Americans?

Rebuilding the ghetto has been viewed as largely a problem for Federal and local governments. However, private business has become more and more aware that it has a vast stake in the elimination of slums. As a result, private industry has increasingly sought to do what it can to rebuild the ghetto.

13

How Business Is Helping to Rebuild Cities

by THE EDITORS OF
U.S. News & World Report

INDUSTRY is jumping into the business of rebuilding U.S. cities in a big way.

A few large companies have been involved for some years in building projects in big cities. Now, suddenly, these few are being joined by many others —banks, insurance companies, railroads, makers of varied products from machine tools to greeting cards.

The sums invested range from a few thousand

From "How Business Is Helping to Rebuild Cities," *U.S. News & World Report,* March 20, 1967, pp. 90–95. Copyright © 1967 by *U.S. News & World Report.* Reprinted by permission.

Who should be responsible for rebuilding city slums—the government, private industry, or both?   (Joe Molnar)

dollars in some cases to scores of millions in others. These are investments that represent new construction or rehabilitation that would otherwise not be done.

There is a growing conviction in Washington, and in city halls, that billions in private capital will be needed to rescue cities from decay—that the job is too big for just the government and the usual real estate developers.

Companies all across the country are pitching in to help. The reasons:

1. To make money. With land values in seemingly endless uptrend, tracts of land given over to new . . . hotels and apartments tend to pile up profits automatically as years go by.

2. To try out new products and new building methods. This is a prime consideration of makers

of aluminum, floor and ceiling tiles, wallboard—key products of some companies now plunging into the rebuilding business.

3. To improve neighborhoods in which the companies operate or from which they draw workers. A drug company, a machine tool company, a greeting card company were led into urban renewal by thinking along this line.

4. To make a productive asset out of unused or little used space. Railroad tracks, eyesores in many areas, are being covered over with handsome new developments—new sources of income for the railroads, assets for the cities in which they operate.

Interest in Renewal

For one thing, there is growing interest in fixing up run-down tenements and row houses in the slums. Dozens of firms are becoming involved in this side of urban renewal.

One reason for this interest: New financing arrangements offer companies a chance to make a "limited" profit on buildings bought, renovated and then sold to local housing agencies or non-profit groups, under supervision of the Federal Housing Administration.

U.S. Gypsum is investing 1.6 million dollars in six tenements in New York's Harlem and plans to put 1.2 million into six more in the Hough district of Cleveland. The tenements are gutted, rebuilt inside, spruced up outside, then rented back to the original tenants.

In the process, U.S. Gypsum hopes to interest many building contractors by showing them there is a reasonable profit to be made in this work. The company also gets a chance to try out new products and processes—a new electric heating system, a floor-leveling material, new paints, new panels.

Manhattan Project

In New York seven big banks are lending money, on "favorable" terms, for the rehabilitation of 55 five-story "brownstones" on Manhattan's West Side.

On a smaller scale, the Armstrong Cork Company and Smith, Klein & French Laboratories, in North Philadelphia, and Warner & Swasey, in Cleveland, are putting money into rehabilitation of row houses or apartments. The drug and machine tool companies are anxious to improve the neighborhoods in which they operate.

In Pittsburgh, 26 firms, including such giants as U.S. Steel, Westinghouse Electric, Koppers and Pittsburgh Plate Glass, have invested in an agency known as ACTION-Housing, now rebuilding 22 row houses and financing construction of more than a thousand new town houses and apartments. Plans for a large "consortium"* to rehabilitate up to 5,000 homes in the area are under study.

Two big aluminum companies—Alcoa and Reynolds Metals—probably have sponsored more urban renewal projects than any other firms.

Reynolds says its projects—mainly housing—are intended to turn a profit, show off the company's products, test new ideas, and demonstrate that the firm is doing something to improve living conditions. Reynolds is working on what it calls "the nation's largest urban-renewal project"—10,000 homes plus stores and industrial facilities in Philadelphia. The company will be responsible for about half the job.

---

consortium—a joining together of businesses.

Converted Movie Lot

Alcoa leans to big apartment houses, office buildings, and hotels.

Its biggest project: Century City, now being developed on part of the old Twentieth Century-Fox lot in Los Angeles.

Hallmark Cards got tired of looking at the rundown commercial area near its headquarters in Kansas City, Missouri. With city approval and a tax abatement, the company plans to develop garden apartments, offices, a hotel, two motor inns, concealed parking areas, malls, parks, and plazas, all at a cost of more than 100 million dollars.

Eastwick, just outside of Philadelphia—desolate, rotting houses with an open sewer running behind them. (Reynolds Metals)

Eastwick's town gardens, built by the Reynolds Metals company, are sanitary, comfortable, and attractive. (Lawrence Williams)

Many firms are erecting new headquarters or branch offices, and some are concluding that there is much to be gained by making these buildings part of a larger urban development. Along these lines are the Prudential Center in Boston, being developed by the Prudential Insurance Company of America, and the Financial Plaza of the Pacific sponsored by Castle & Cook, the Bank of Hawaii and other firms in Honolulu.

The railroads are busily promoting the "air rights" over their tracks and stations for modern urban centers—The Pennsylvania Railroad in New York, Philadelphia, Chicago and Pittsburgh; the Il-

LePelley in *Christian Science Monitor* (Boston)
"I don't believe we've really met."

linois Central in Chicago. The "Pennsy" estimates it has put 50 million dollars into this development already and will invest 50 million more.

The question now: Will this stream of private funds swell into a river big enough to save the cities?

FURTHER INQUIRY

1. Why has business become involved in rebuilding slum areas?
2. Which of the reasons listed on pages 132–133 seems most important to you? Why?
3. Can our cities be rebuilt without the help of private enterprise? Give reasons for your answer.
4. Could you suggest other ways in which industry might help to eliminate the slums?
5. If industry contributes to rebuilding the slums, should it be given tax benefits? Why or why not?

Is there anything we can learn about rebuilding slums by studying the "ants"? The author of this selection thinks so. The ants to which he refers are the "Ants of Tokyo." The author draws on his knowledge of a slum in Tokyo, Japan, for such lessons as it may have for the slums of the cities of America.

14

A Lesson from the "Ants"

by EDWARD HIGBEE

IN Tokyo, as in any other city, there are those unlucky but industrious ones who grub a livelihood out of dump heaps. They are the human buzzards, or as Tokyo calls them, the "Ants," who salvage something from their more fortunate brothers' trash. They are ragpickers, tin-can collectors, and waste-paper bundlers who glean, sort, and then sell the stuff to junkyards. The work is hard, demeaning, and filthy, but it returns a subsistence and the city is cleaner because the job is done. Over a

From *The Squeeze: Cities Without Space* by Edward Higbee (New York: William Morrow & Co., 1960), pp. 81–84. Copyright © 1960 by Edward Higbee. Reprinted by permission of William Morrow & Co., Inc.

Community programs using public and private funds are just beginning in most cities. *(Above, left)* In a Harlem street, workers dig holes for some of the 320 trees to be planted as an Up-Lift Project. *(Below, left)* Youngsters help to clear a courtyard of garbage as part of Harlem's Garbage Cleanup. *(Above)* East Harlem welfare families pool their checks to buy food, which they keep in a former candy store. (Wide World)

decade ago, Tokyo's Ants and their families began to assemble their own version of a hobo jungle in a neglected riverside park. Since then this do-it-yourself slum, constructed of whatever castoff materials the Ants could scrounge, has grown into a settlement of three hundred people who have developed a remarkable social security system to care for themselves as well as for their dependent children and aged. Their welfare plan, to which all active Ants contribute a daily pittance, provides free: a modest wedding, medical care, and a funeral when the time comes.

Living quarters in the Ants' community, while they look like hovels, are kept as neat as possible, and there is a common bathhouse in daily operation so that all who return from their dirty tasks may enjoy the pleasure and cleanliness it offers. Now the Ants have had enough of mean surroundings and they are engaged in an urban renewal program financed by themselves. They have saved money and have won respect for their thrift and efforts to live decently. The City of Tokyo has given them permission to buy five acres of waterfront land where they will build a new community with modest apartments, a dining hall, a nursery, a bathhouse, and a church. Their master plan reserves space for recreation areas and for a community livestock project of a thousand chickens and twenty pigs. The Ants, who have lived long enough in the lower depths, intend to become people.

As the Ants have demonstrated, slums are a matter of culture as well as of economics. If people possess a taste for decency, no matter how mean their circumstances may be, they will improve their environment. If they lack culture they will defile and degrade whatever place they occupy, even though it be a suite at the Waldorf. However, much as the Ants may have wanted a better life, that would have been impossible for them until they had saved the wherewithal to buy it. The surge toward civil betterment which is now growing in urban America indicates that the city, far from being moribund,* has within it a remarkable desire to improve. It has the culture. But to succeed the city also needs a means by which people can rehabilitate themselves, and that is a far more complex problem than urban renewal. It is wishful thinking to believe that the current wave of slum clearance, which is strictly a real estate construction program, will in any way solve the far more difficult social task which is raised by the slum dwellers themselves. The two objectives should not be confused; otherwise the real, but distinctly limited, possibilities for improvement of the

---

moribund—almost dead.

1147 *Urban League of Greater New York* **1147**

A street academy sponsored by Union Carbide is one step toward providing the culture as well as the economic means to reverse the urban blight. (Shalmon Bernstein)

city's physical plant may be dissipated by presuming that it has welfare objectives that the program cannot possibly achieve.

In the long run, it would probably be better for any city to undertake fewer urban renewal projects and to concentrate on doing those so tastefully that they would bring the middle class back to town. This is not to deny that the inhabitants of slums need better living quarters, but as the program now operates, the truly indigent are not aided by urban renewal, and many of them are made more miserable by being uprooted and driven from their familiar neighborhoods into other districts where they have no ties or affections. Since the rents in renewal-project buildings are far beyond the means of most slum dwellers, the people who do move into the new apartments are generally of modest but independent means who come from decent but underprivileged neighborhoods where they have been living in old but respectable buildings. On the whole, they are people who cannot afford the suburbs but

143

do not have to live in slums. The places they vacate then may be overrun in turn by slum D.P.'s* who double up to save on rents. Such is the pecking order in the urban barnyard. It results in a lot of demolition and reconstruction but is no basic solution to the problem of degraded neighborhoods.

Most of the modern city's present slums are in what once were, and still could be, privileged neighborhoods. The West Side of New York, which only in the last decade has become as crowded and filthy as Harlem, is, from the standpoint of location, the best residential district in the city. Even now a very large percentage of existing buildings would make choice residences. Many were once the homes and apartments of the well-to-do and have real charm which would be a credit in any age to any city. Almost every city with slums can point to similarly well-situated neighborhoods with good buildings which have gone to pot only through misuse. The kind of urban renewal which simply destroys the old to put up the new does not correct the cultural depravity that creates slums. It only scatters the seed.

FURTHER INQUIRY

1. Why does the author say that slums are a matter of culture as well as of economics?
2. Why does the author feel that urban renewal is not the basic solution to the problem of slums? Do you agree or disagree? Why?
3. What changes a neighborhood from a privileged one to a slum?
4. How is the city of Tokyo providing for its Ants? Might other cities do the same?

D.P.'s—displaced persons.

In this selection, the prominent executive director of the National Urban
League presents his views on who is
responsible for decent housing and
suggests some of the ways in which it
may be achieved. He says that decent
housing for all is the keystone of a
healthy democracy. Do you agree or
disagree with him? Why or why not?

15

Decent Housing:
Whose
Responsibility?

by WHITNEY M. YOUNG, JR.

IN this latter half of the Twentieth Century in
America, decent housing for all is one of the keystones to a healthy democracy, assuring each individual an opportunity for reaching his maximum
potential. We are all victims of the tragic consequences of turning our backs for generations on

From *To Be Equal* by Whitney M. Young, Jr. (New York:
McGraw-Hill Book Co., 1964), pp. 157–58. Copyright © 1964 by
Whitney M. Young, Jr. Used by permission of McGraw-Hill
Book Co.

Children of the slums read about the world beyond the inner city. But they may never become a part of that world. (OEO)

"WE HAVE A DREAM"

OUT OF OUR PAIN COMES WISDOM

RICH OF 102 • WALDA OF 102
CHANCY & Arlene LOVE

(Joe Molnar)

this necessity. When the TV and press bannerline the news of school boycotts, rent strikes, delinquency, gang warfare, mugging, murder, and mayhem, keep in mind that the crime of inadequate shelter provides one of the sustaining chords in this modern symphony of discord. For those who doubt this, I merely refer to the . . . charts so dear to the urban renewal exponents. These highlight the high-incidence areas of crime, ill-health, poverty, inferior educational attainment, unemployment, and decrepit housing. The charts paint a multi-colored bullseye on each ghetto slum area.

I am at a loss to understand how intelligent, enlightened, big business continues to stand silently by and observe calmly the occupation of the central city by the lowest income groups. This has not only serious economic implications in terms of its investment and low tax return, but, if this is a homogeneous racial bloc, it also has meaningful political significance. These reasons alone—aside from any humane considerations—should make these business-men our most articulate spokesmen for open oc-cupancy and racial dispersion.

The future of our cities and the larger community depends in large measure on effective desegregation of neighborhoods and of the shelter supply in general. Until large-scale progress is made, the problems of segregated schools and public accommodations will continue. We need a common market in housing for a healthy national economy just as a common market is necessary for a healthy international economy. Negro families want to bid into such a market without racial restriction. Their needs and interests, AS THEY SEE THEM, and their financial capacity should be the only criteria for any Americans to secure decent housing. Segregated shelter is a negative luxury no nation is rich enough nor strong enough to afford.

FURTHER INQUIRY

1. Why does the author say that "decent housing for all is one of the keystones to a healthy democracy"?
2. What does the author mean by a "common market" in housing?
3. Why does he say that segregated housing is something no nation can afford?
4. In your view, who has the major responsibility for providing decent housing for all? Why?

Notes

Suggestions for Additional Reading

Index

Notes

THE PROBLEM AND THE CHALLENGE

1. Michael Harrington, *The Other America* (Baltimore: Penguin Books, 1964), p. 12.
2. Daniel Seligman, "The Enduring Slums," in *The Expanding Metropolis* (New York: Doubleday Anchor Books, 1958), p. 96.
3. Kenneth Clark, *Dark Ghetto* (New York: Harper & Row, 1965), p. 66.
4. Raymond Vernon, *The Myth and Reality of Our Urban Problems* (Cambridge, Mass.: Harvard University Press, 1966), pp. 68–70.
5. *Ibid.*, p. 70.
6. Oscar H. Steiner, *Downtown USA* (Dobbs Ferry, N.Y.: Oceana Publications, 1964), p. 4.
7. *Ibid.*
8. David R. Hunter, *The Slums: Challenge and Response* (New York: Free Press of Glencoe, 1964), p. 15.
9. Office of Economic Opportunity, "Community Action and Urban Housing," *Community Action,* November, 1967, p. 10.
10. Oscar H. Steiner, *Our Housing Jungle— and Your Pocketbook* (New York: University Publishers, 1960), p. 44.
11. Robert C. Weaver, *The Urban Complex* (New York: Doubleday Anchor Books, 1966), p. 126.

12. Seligman, *op. cit.*, p. 102.

13. *Ibid.*, p. 107.

14. *Ibid.*

15. Steiner, *Downtown USA*, p. 63.

16. *Ibid.*, p. 64.

Suggestions for Additional Reading

1. BANFIELD, EDWARD C. *Politics, Planning and the Public Interest.* New York: The Free Press of Glencoe, 1955. Here the author discusses the importance of city planning and its relationship to the public interest on the one hand and political urban realities on the other.

2. HUNTER, DAVID R. *The Slums: Challenge and Response.* New York: The Free Press of Glencoe, 1964. The author examines the challenge posed by slums to modern urban living together with the answers that have thus far been put forth.

3. LAURENTI, LUIGI. *Property Values and Race.* Berkeley: University of California Press, 1960. This is a definitive study of the effect of color upon property values. The author concludes, ". . . non-white occupancy does not necessarily adversely influence property values."

4. NATIONAL COMMITTEE AGAINST DISCRIMINATION IN HOUSING. *How the Federal Government Builds Ghettoes.* New York: National Committee Against Discrimination in Housing, 1968.

In its introduction the report states, "This pamphlet constitutes a charge . . . that the Federal Government builds ghettoes." The pamphlet must be read in order to ascertain for oneself the truth or falsity of the charge.

5. STEINER, OSCAR H. *Downtown USA*. Dobbs Ferry, N.Y.: Oceana Publishers, Inc., 1964. In this book the author describes the deterioration that has taken place in the downtown sections of most cities.

6. STEINER, OSCAR H. *Our Housing Jungle—and Your Pocketbook*. New York: University Publishers, Inc., 1960. This book describes the difficulty the black man encounters when trying to buy a home on anything resembling equal terms with the white man.

7. TEBBEL, ROBERT. *The Slum Makers*. New York: The Dial Press, 1963. Here the author develops those factors that contribute to the making of slums and inveighs against those interests that are responsible for their creation.

8. VERNON, RAYMOND. *The Myth and Reality of Our Urban Problems*. Cambridge, Mass.: Harvard University Press, 1966. This urbanologist takes a close look at urban problems, in particular those having to do with housing, and places them in perspective.

9. WEAVER, ROBERT C. *The Urban Complex*. Garden City, N.Y.: Doubleday Anchor Books, 1966. The former Secretary of the Department of Housing and Urban Development writes of

the complexities of urban renewal and relates them to problems of transportation, housing, and ghetto life.

10. WEAVER, ROBERT C. *The Negro Ghetto*. New York: Harcourt, Brace & Co., 1948. This is an early study of the nature of the black ghetto in relation to urban renewal and redevelopment.

Index